MW00356256

EMOTIONS

What Are They and What We Do With Them

Rick Sizemore

TALL WOOD
PUBLISHING HOUSE

Tall Wood Publishing House
PO Box 8
Pembroke, Virginia 24136

Unless otherwise noted, Scripture quotations are taken from the New American Standard Bible®, Copyright © 1960, 1962, 1963, 1968, 1971, 1972, 1973, 1975, 1977, 1995 by The Lockman Foundation. Used by permission. (www.lockman.org)

ISBN 13: 978-1-57688-070-8 (print)
ISBN 13: 978-1-57688-071-5 (ebook)

Printed in the United States of America.

This book is dedicated to God,
who created us with amazing emotions,
and to Paula, my beloved wife,
who has faithfully loved me for
the last thirty-five years of our marriage.

Acknowledgments

This revised edition has come about as a result of changes and observations in the writing part of my life over the last several years. I would be amiss to say that many people have played an intricate role in bringing this book to life the first time around. I would like to mention one particular lady who was both a cheerleader and the main component in getting the first edition of this book and the Dealing Jesus website through the first phases of production and completion. This special lady was Jennifer Cesario who is now with Jesus. She is sorely missed but her perky laugher still rings clear in my memories.

The folks who were an intricate part of the first edition are:

My wife, Paula; Zach Williams, Crystal Vitelli, and the Venveo staff; Rob Agnew; Tullio O'Reilly; Mitch and Leigha Semones; The elders of Dwelling Place NRV, SML, BSG, and ATL; all the main body of believers at Dwelling Place Christian Fellowship in Christiansburg, Virginia. All of you have been an inspiration to my heart these last fourteen years.

Rick Sizemore

Table of Contents

Preface

When our children were young, Paula and I enjoyed taking them to a number of different museums. One museum that sticks out in my mind had several exhibits that asked me to insert my hand into a closed metal box. The box contained objects of different substances and shapes, and the purpose was to see if I could identify the objects by feel, not by sight. So every time I inserted my hand into the box, this question rang through my mind: What am I feeling?

We ask ourselves that question every day. Commonly, it is followed by, Why am I feeling this way? In some Christian circles, the presence of these questions has come to be considered a sign of immaturity. We are inadvertently trained to think in ways that are contrary to Scripture:

> If I were stronger in my faith, I wouldn't feel this way.

> God is bigger than what I am feeling, so I just need to ignore this!

> If I am not full of joy all the time, there must be something wrong with me.

The Word of God teaches that our emotions can help direct our lives. The questions What am I feeling? and Why am I feeling this way? need to be answered, not because the person who asks them "needs help" but because emotions are God-given gifts purposed to help us live life to its fullest.

The Lord wants us to be able to use our emotions in a healthy way. He created us with the beautiful capacity to feel, and He also gave us the ability to monitor and implement what we are feeling. When we understand His design for emotions, we can allow His Word to train our hearts to discern what a particular emotion is signaling. We then can respond accordingly.

For years, a friend of mine thought she was emotionally unstable because of all the things she was feeling when she went to church. But as she began to understand what she was feeling and what those emotions signaled, she realized what God was doing in her, and her soul was filled with peace. In addition, her church was blessed by the revelations God gave her—revelations that came through what she was feeling. Emotions truly are a gift from God. When we understand what is being signaled within us and how to respond to that signal, it can result in life and freedom.

This book is written from a pastoral perspective, seeking to give some understanding to the whys and the whats of the emotions we all experience. It should not be considered a scientific study of emotions but a ministerial study. We will take an in-depth look at emotions, their origins, what Scripture has to say about them, and how we should respond to them.

If you are someone who doesn't feel, you may want to start reading at Chapter 2, which talks about what to do if your emotions have been shut down.

PART ONE

God Created You To Feel

"At that very time He rejoiced greatly in the Holy Spirit, and said, 'I praise You, O Father, Lord of heaven and earth, that You have hidden these things from the wise and intelligent and have revealed them to infants. Yes, Father, for this way was well-pleasing in Your sight.'"

— Luke 10:21

Many of us were trained to be skeptical of what we feel, but God created us with emotions—He created us to feel. When we learn how to discern what we are feeling, we will be able to interact with Him and the world in the full, healthy way He intended.

1 An Introduction to Emotions

Emotions are one of the most controversial subjects in the Christian world. Half of the Body of Christ will discount anything that appears to be emotional, while the other half of the Body of Christ will not even listen to a sermon unless that sermon appeals to their emotions.

In between these two extremes are dozens of other variations. Clearly, the Church of Jesus Christ is very diverse in its opinions.

The main problem with emotions is that the Church does not understand them — yet that should not disqualify them.

We need to understand emotions in order to appropriately interact with the world around us and fully interact with God.

Emotions Defined

The terms emotion and feeling are virtually interchangeable.

In fact, *The Merriam-Webster Dictionary* uses each term to define the other:

Feeling: an emotional state or reaction
plural: susceptibility to impression: sensitivity
(the remark hurt her feelings)

Emotion: the affective aspect of consciousness: feeling
a: a state of feeling
b: a psychic and physical reaction (as anger or fear) sub-
jectively experienced as strong feeling and physiologically
involving changes that prepare the body for immediate
vigorous action

Notice that the above definition for emotion mentions the
psychic (or soulish) reaction and the physical reaction. The
traditional definition of the soul is the mind, will, and emotions, but according to Scripture, we can experience physical
emotions as well as spiritual emotions. The emotional signals
produced by the body are different from the emotional signals produced by the soul, just as the spirit's emotions signal
something different than the body's emotions. We will look
at all three types of emotions in this book, and this will be our
working definition of the topic:

Emotions are the result of an event that has taken place, is
taking place, or will take place. For example, when a woman
experiences birth pains, those pains signal something that is
about to occur: the birth of a child.

> *"Whenever a woman is in labor **she has pain, because
> her hour has come**; but when she gives birth to the child,
> she no longer remembers the anguish because of the joy
> that a child has been born into the world."*
> — John 16:21, (emphasis added)

The feeling is not a negative thing—it is a signal, or indicator, that something is happening. If I hit my finger with a
hammer, the pain I feel is a signal of the event. The pain is
not the problem; the pain is the result of the injury. If we had
no feelings of pain, how would we know when something

happened to us or that something was going wrong in our bodies?

An emotion is a signal of an event.

In the same way, an emotion can also be a signal of a spiritual or soulish event. One of the most important emotions is love. Some claim that love is not actually an emotion but a choice. That can be partially true, especially in the beginning, but it is much more than a choice as well. Love can be sensed in all three parts of our being: body, soul, and spirit. When they are near those they love or feel attracted to, some people describe the feeling as "butterflies" in the pit of the stomach — this is the physical emotion of love. The soul (the mind and heart) senses the physical attraction and is drawn to spend time with that other person. The human spirit is the conduit through which we can sense God's love the most. Love, in its richest form, is an emotion that carries us over the obstacles and chasms that would hinder us from attaining fullness in our relationships.

Three times in Scripture the Lord commands husbands to love their wives, and within the sphere of the Law of the Spirit of Life,[1] those commands are creative words. When God gives a command in His Word, it is to impart life and transforming power; He does not command and then expect us to perform that command on our own. He commands that we may receive His words by faith and walk in the reality of what we believe.[2] So when God commands us to love, He is imparting to us the ability to love through the power of His Word and the Holy Spirit. Husbands have a commanded destiny to love their wives like Jesus loves the Church. There is no way we could ever perform to that standard in the natural. Only the power of God's Word and the Holy Spirit could cause us, as human beings, to love as Jesus loves.[3]

Love is a very strong emotion that God uses to signal to us whom we are to marry. Without the emotion of love, who would want to live intimately with another person? But when we have love for a particular person, that emotion fills our hearts. The emotion of love signals to us that we have found someone we want to spend the rest of our lives with.[4] If there were no feeling of love, most relationships would dissolve.

It Is All Right to Feel

The simple problem with emotions is that we often do not understand them—but that does not mean we have to discount them. When we feel something, we need to understand where, what, and why we are feeling it.

Before we can understand these details, however, we first must understand that it is all right to feel and experience emotions. Many of us have come to believe we cannot trust our feelings, but that belief is based on a lack of knowledge, which can have serious consequences.[5] If we do not know what we are feeling or how to respond to what we are feeling, we could either discount the emotion or possibly be led off into some type of destructive reaction. Both discounting the emotion and responding poorly to it could have weighty results. For example, if a person were experiencing intense stomach cramps and did not understand that the pain was due to a ruptured appendix, the results could be catastrophic.

We answer the where, what, and why of certain emotions on a daily basis without realizing it. If I put my hand on a hot stove, I need to register that pain so I can move my hand! If I do not comprehend that my hand is burning, how will I know to pull my hand away? This specific feeling of pain is important for a healthy physical existence.

When I go to the doctor, he often asks me, "What are you feeling?" Or, "Does anything hurt?" The doctor uses physical feelings, the emotions of the body, as indicators of events in my body. The feeling itself is not a negative or harmful thing; it is merely a signal of a physical occurrence—something is happening inside me, and I can feel it.

I often witness people getting mad at themselves because

they feel something. My conviction is that we simply need to understand what the emotion is signaling and then take the appropriate action.

In this book, we will look at each facet of our being — spirit, soul, and body — and the events that can generate emotions within us. We will then examine the response each type of emotion should receive. When we know what we are feeling, where it came from, and why we are feeling it, we will value how God created us, instead of discounting His work. We will know how to respond to the emotional signals we are sensing.

Jesus and Emotions

Even though we are trained in many Christian circles to be skeptical of our emotions, Scripture clearly shows the legitimacy of listening and responding to them. Let's look at the emotions of the most balanced Person to walk the earth: Jesus Christ.

We are called to walk as Jesus walked: *"For you have been called for this purpose, since Christ also suffered for you, leaving you an example for you to follow in His steps"* (1 Peter 2:21). Jesus lived His physical life with a great deal of emotion. He did not let those emotions drive Him, but He understood what emotions are, and as a result, He used them in His own life and as He ministered to others. If He experienced and subsequently expressed emotion, it is important for us to do the same.

Jesus Was Tired and Weary

Every person knows what it is like to feel tired and weary. While on earth, Jesus subjected Himself to the same physical emotions of tiredness we feel:

> *"So He came to a city of Samaria called Sychar, near the parcel of ground that Jacob gave to his son Joseph; and Jacob's well was there. So Jesus, **being wearied from His journey**, was sitting thus by the well. It was about the sixth hour. There came a woman of Samaria to draw water. Jesus said to her, 'Give Me a drink.' For His disciples had gone away into the city to buy food."*
>
> — John 4:5–8, (emphasis added)

Being tired and weary is a physical emotion that signals the body needs rest and refreshment. When Jesus was tired, He heeded the emotion by seeking what He needed: food and water. At the same time, however, He did not allow His weariness to direct His thinking. That is where many of us fall into trouble — we allow our physical emotions to direct our thoughts, instead of understanding them in a way that helps us continue moving forward. Even though He was physically tired in John 4, Jesus still sought to minister His Father's love to a hurting and broken woman.

Jesus Experienced Joy

Jesus was free to express great joy during His life on earth. The Bible says He "rejoiced greatly":

> *"At that very time He rejoiced greatly in the Holy Spirit, and said, 'I praise You, O Father, Lord of heaven and earth, that You have hidden these things from the wise and intelligent and have revealed them to infants. Yes, Father, for this way was well-pleasing in Your sight.'"*
>
> — Luke 10:21

According to Spiros Zodhiates[A], the Greek word for "rejoiced greatly" literally means "to leap; to exult, leap for joy, to show one's joy by leaping and skipping, denoting excessive or ecstatic joy and delight." In other words, as Jesus praised His Father, He jumped around in joy over the things the dis-

20

ciples were learning.

But even though He felt extreme happiness and expressed His joy, He did not allow the expression of His emotions to distract Him from His objective. In the midst of His joy, He directed His disciples toward the more important thing. It was excellent that the demons submitted to them in His name, but it was better that their names were written in God's Book of Life.

Jesus Experienced Grief and Sorrow

When Jesus arrived at the funeral of His good friend Lazarus, He saw the man's sisters, Mary and Martha, and expressed deep sorrow:

> *"When Jesus therefore saw her weeping, and the Jews who came with her also weeping, He was **deeply moved in spirit** and was troubled, and said, 'Where have you laid him?' They said to Him, 'Lord, come and see.' Jesus wept."* — John 11:33–35, (emphasis added)

Many people — men, in particular — have a hard time showing sorrow, but Jesus was free to cry intensely with His friends. An interesting thing in John 11 is that He knew He was about to raise Lazarus from the dead, but He still showed empathy toward Mary and Martha.

He was "deeply moved in spirit" and "was troubled," but He did not lose His focus. The sorrow did not overcome Him. He still ministered with power and called Lazarus out of the tomb (verse 43).

Jesus Experienced Love and Compassion

We also see Jesus feeling love and compassion. When the rich young ruler asked Him about obtaining eternal life, Jesus felt a sincere love for the man:

> *"And he said to Him, 'Teacher, I have kept all these things from my youth up.' Looking at him, Jesus felt a love for him and said to him, 'One thing you lack: go and sell all you possess and give to the poor, and you will have treasure in heaven; and come, follow Me.' But at these words he was saddened, and he went away grieving, for he was one who owned much property."* — Mark 10:20–22

In this passage, Jesus experienced emotion and used that emotion to direct His ministry. He genuinely loved the rich young ruler who stood before Him, but His love was filled with knowledge and discernment—He let the ruler walk away. He knew what was best for that man.

Jesus Experienced Anger

Anger is a natural emotion that typically occurs in response to what is perceived to be an unjust event.

> *"They were watching Him to see if He would heal him on the Sabbath, so that they might accuse Him. He said to the man with the withered hand, 'Get up and come forward!' And He said to them, 'Is it lawful to do good or to do harm on the Sabbath, to save a life or to kill?' But they kept silent. After looking around at them with anger, grieved at their hardness of heart, He said to the man, 'Stretch out your hand.' And he stretched it out, and his hand was restored."* — Mark 3:2–5

Jesus' emotion of anger arose from an emotion of grief. He saw the hardness of the Pharisees' hearts and the results of men allowing religion to dominate their lives. Many times when we become angry, we sin or cause others pain, but when Jesus became angry, He healed. Even though He was upset at the Pharisees' hard-heartedness, He remained focused on the task at hand.

Jesus Experienced Stress

In the Garden of Gethsemane before His crucifixion, Jesus took on all the sin, pain, sickness, and sorrow of this world.[6] The pressure of that process was emotionally traumatic for Him:

> *"And He took with Him Peter and the two sons of Zebedee, and began to be grieved and distressed. Then He said to them, 'My soul is deeply grieved, to the point of death; remain here and keep watch with Me.'"*
> — Matthew 26:37–38

In the first verse, Matthew described Jesus as being grieved and distressed. In the next verse, Jesus did two important things. First, He shared with the disciples the degree of the emotional stress He was carrying. He was free to express His emotions to others, while many of us have a hard time expressing what we truly feel.

The second important thing Jesus did was ask the disciples to stand with Him in the midst of the emotional storm. In Scripture, the word comfort comes from the Greek word paraklesis, which literally means "called alongside." So Jesus was asking the disciples to stand alongside Him in the moment of His greatest stress — He was asking for comfort.

A few years ago when I was in Amman, Jordan, I became very sick. My friend Najeeb Sadoras simply sat by my bed and prayed for me. His actions were a tremendous comfort and blessing to my heart. That was what Jesus was crying out for — for His brothers to be alongside Him. They couldn't ease the pain He was feeling, but they could be with Him. That is comfort. With this understanding of the word comfort, it is interesting to me that the Holy Spirit is called the Comforter.

In Hebrews 5:7, we see another description of Jesus in the Garden of Gethsemane that night, weeping as He prayed to His Father:

"In the days of His flesh, He offered up both prayers and supplications with loud crying and tears to the One able to save Him from death, and He was heard because of His piety."

Even though Jesus was praying with intense sorrow, He did not lose a reverent attitude toward His Father. He understood what He was feeling, and He responded in an appropriate manner, which resulted in life: God heard His cries.

So, as we have just seen, Jesus, God in the flesh, displayed different types of emotions. He experienced great joy, grief, sorrow, anger, love, and compassion. In a larger measure than any of us has ever endured, He also experienced the emotional trauma that sin and death can bring to us in this world. In all of these emotions, He had understanding; He knew what He was feeling and took the appropriate actions. He did not allow any of these emotions to direct Him to inappropriate thinking or responses. Instead, He used them in His personal life and when He ministered to others. We can learn to do the same.

The Creator of Emotion

*"For everyone who partakes only of milk is not accustomed to the word of righteousness, for he is an infant. But solid food is for the mature, who because of practice have **their senses trained to discern good and evil**."*
— Hebrews 5:13–14, (emphasis added)

Whenever we feel an emotion, we first need to determine if it is a physical, soulish, or spiritual emotion. To do this, we need to answer two questions:

What is the emotion signaling?

How do I respond to the emotion?

If we can answer these questions with God's truth, we are set free to feel, to understand what we are feeling, and to know how we should respond to what we are feeling.

Two Ways to Judge the Truth of Your Emotions

Our heavenly Father's heart is that we understand and discern everything going on in and around us. So with any emotion, one of the very first things we need to know is whether or not that emotion is signaling a truth to us. How do we know that what we are feeling is based in truth? We need a foundation on which to judge (discern) what is truth and what is not truth.

God gave us two resources with which to monitor truth within us. The first resource is His Word: *"Sanctify them in the truth; Your word is truth"* (John 17:17). The second gauge of truth is the Holy Spirit: *"When He, the Spirit of truth, comes, He will guide you into all the truth"* (John 16:13). The Holy Spirit and the Word of God are always in agreement with one another. God's Word will not violate the Holy Spirit, and the Holy Spirit will not reveal anything contrary to the truth of God's Word.[7] There is a clear connection, and reliance, between the Holy Spirit and God's Word.

God's Word Judges Emotions

> *"For the word of God is living and active and sharper than any two-edged sword, and piercing as far as the division of soul and spirit, of both joints and marrow, and able to judge the thoughts and intentions of the heart."*
> — Hebrews 4:12

God gives us His Word to explain and monitor what we think and feel. If we feel something that is not in line with His Word, the emotion is signaling something to us that is not truth. The following verses are just a few examples of how we can use God's Word to evaluate what we are feeling:

> If I feel passive and like I just do not care, that emotion is not truth because 2 Timothy 1:7 tells me, *"For God has not given us a spirit of timidity [passivity], but of power and love and discipline."*

> If I feel the emotion of hate, I am feeling an emotion that is not from God because 1 John 2:11 tells me, *"The one who hates his brother is in the darkness and walks in the darkness, and does not know where he is going because the darkness has blinded his eyes."*

> If I am worried or suffering from anxiety, it is a signal that something is not right in my soul: *"For this reason I say to you, do not be worried about your life, as to what you will eat or what you will drink; nor for your body, as to what you will put on"* (Matthew 6:25).

> If I lose my peace, my heart and mind are being distracted from the Lord: *"The steadfast of mind You will keep in perfect peace, because he trusts in You"* (Isaiah 26:3).

> If I am feeling spiritually weak, I have lost the joy of the Lord: *"The joy of the Lord is your strength."* (Nehemiah 8:10).[B]

A few years ago, a young couple came to me and said, "We believe God is telling us to get married right now."

I asked them why they wanted to get married. They told me they were in love with each other, and I then asked what their parents had to say about it.

"Our parents want us to wait, but we believe we should go ahead and get married," they replied.

That told me everything I needed to know, and I was unable to give them the answer they wanted. "You guys aren't in love with each other," I told them. "You're in lust with each other."

As you may imagine, that offended them. "How can you say that to us?"

I reminded them of what Paul wrote in Galatians 5:22–23: *"The fruit of the Spirit is love, joy, peace, patience, kindness, goodness, faithfulness, gentleness, self-control; against such things there is no law."* The Greek word for fruit is singular, not plural. My understanding is that there are not nine different fruits — there is one fruit, and that one fruit has nine different facets. So we cannot have the love of the Spirit without peace. We cannot have the love of the Spirit without joy. The real kicker in their situation was that we can't have the love of the Spirit without patience. The moment they told me they could not wait to be married, even when the authorities in their lives instructed them to wait, I knew the emotion they thought was love was not the love of the Spirit.

They decided to heed my counsel and wait, and the end of the story is that they broke up and married other people. If they had gone ahead and married one another, they would have missed God's best for them. Obviously, I am not saying that every couple who marries quickly is out of step with God's will, but in this specific situation, the evidence of the fruit of the Spirit was not apparent in the couple's decision to get married.

On another occasion, a man came up to me and told me he had peace about leaving his wife and marrying his secretary. But peace from the Spirit of God has self-control, and it will not violate His Word, which declares that divorce and adultery are sin. Therefore, this man's sense of peace was not from the Spirit; it was a soulish peace that comes from not having to face and work through problems.

In summary, God's Word enables us to judge our emotions. If we feel something that is not in line with His Word, that emotion is not telling us the truth.

The Holy Spirit Judges Emotions

We need the Word of God to be the gauge of what we feel and whether or not that feeling is based on truth. Whenever we use the Word of God in this way, we need the Holy Spirit's emotions to monitor our reception and application of that truth.

The nine facets of the fruit of the Spirit are actually spiritual emotions of truth. Even though love, joy, peace, and patience are more than simple feelings, we can definitely sense them when we are flowing in them. If I have love of the Spirit, I will also have joy and peace of the Spirit. I think of this like an orange and its different sections. It is all the same orange, but with the fruit of the Spirit, each "section" of that orange manifests itself differently. We cannot have just one of the facets without the others. These emotions are signals to us that we are walking in the Spirit.[8]

Paul tells us to allow the "peace of Christ" to rule or, literally, to umpire or referee in our hearts.[9] In other words, we are to use the spiritual emotion of peace to help us direct the flow of our lives. We will talk more about spiritual emotions in a later chapter; for now, we need to understand that we should use the Holy Spirit's emotions listed in Galatians 5 to gauge how we receive and speak the truth of God's Word.

The Pharisees knew God's Word, but they often did not speak and act in His truth, even though they spoke and acted on His Word. Jesus rebuked them because they tried to live spiritual lives without the spiritual emotion of love judging their actions:

> "But woe to you Pharisees! For you pay tithe of mint and rue and every kind of garden herb, and yet disregard jus-

*tice and **the love of God**; but these are the things you should have done without neglecting the others."*
— Luke 11:42, (emphasis added)

The apostle Paul also exhorts us to gauge our hearts with God's truth and the spiritual emotion of love when we speak.[10] When I preach, I use love as a gauge to test my heart and my message. I ask myself, Am I speaking the Word of God in love and humility? Like the Pharisees, we can find ourselves speaking His Word without love and humility; in those moments, we are not speaking it in the Spirit. God's Word is truth—yet we fail to speak the fullness of truth if we are not speaking His Word in love. Agape love (described in 1 Corinthians 13:4–8) is from God, and it is a spiritual emotion.

James addresses this issue when he differentiates between wisdom from above and wisdom that is earthly, soulish, or demonic.[11] He tells us to look for the spiritual emotions of the fruit of the Spirit: *"The wisdom from above is first pure, then peaceable, gentle . . ."* Based on that statement, we know that God's wisdom will be accompanied by purity, peace, and gentleness.

James also tells us to look for the negative spiritual emotions of jealousy and disorder (though disorder is not an emotion, we can feel the emotions associated with disorder). In fact, he says if we sense jealousy or selfish ambition in our hearts, we should not even speak. When those things are present within us and we do speak, we lie against God's truth. If we speak God's Word outside the nature and character of who God is, we communicate things that are contrary to the fullness of His truth. We can speak God's Word without speaking His truth in the Spirit.

I have attended numerous religious meetings in which I could sense confusion and disorder in the room as people discussed different issues. Those feelings are negative spiritual emotions that often signal the presence of ungodly wisdom. If disorder is present when I am speaking, I could be operating out of a personal state of jealousy and selfish ambition. It is for this reason John tells us to test the spirit of the person who is speaking:

> *"Beloved, do not believe every spirit, but test the spirits to see whether they are from God, because many false prophets have gone out into the world."* — 1 John 4:1

Our emotions are one of the main ways we test a speaker's spirit. Are we feeling love and peace, or are we feeling judgment, control, condemnation, confusion, or selfish ambition? Whenever we speak God's Word, we want to be speaking that Word in and by His Spirit.

When we speak God's Word from the flow of His Spirit, the results are His love, joy, and peace. We, and those to whom we are speaking, can feel the sweetness of fellowship with God and one another. We can feel what God is doing. Emotions are a great gift that can help lead us in our walk with God.

Key Points of Chapter 1

What Do We Do with Emotions?

Whenever we feel an emotion, we first need to determine if it is a physical, soulish, or spiritual emotion. To do this, we need to answer the following two questions:

What is the emotion signaling?

How do I respond to the emotion?

If we can answer these questions with God's truth, we are set free to feel, to understand what we are feeling, and to know how to respond to what we are feeling.

How Do We Discern What We Are Feeling?

With any emotion, one of the very first things we need to know is whether or not that emotion is signaling a truth to us. God gave us two resources to monitor truth within us: His Word[12] and the Holy Spirit.[13] The Holy Spirit and the Word of God are always in agreement with one another. God's Word will not violate the Holy Spirit, and the Holy Spirit will not reveal anything that is contrary to the truth of God's Word.

We need the Word of God to be the gauge of what we feel and whether or not that feeling is based on truth. We then need the

Holy Spirit's emotions to monitor our reception and application of that truth.

Notes / Reference Scriptures

[A] The Complete Word Study Dictionary: New Testament, Chattanooga: AMG International, Inc. 1993

[B] If you are unable to accept the truth in these areas, don't be alarmed. It is merely a signal that something is hindering you, and that can be remedied through God's mercy and grace. Visit www.dealingjesus.org for more information.

1. John 8:2
2. 1 Thessalonians 2:13
3. Romans 5:5
4. Ecclesiastes 9:9
5. Isaiah 5:13; Hosea 4:6
6. Isaiah 53:4-6
7. Psalm 119:160
8. Galatians 5:16-27
9. Colossians 3:15
10. Ephesians 4:15
11. James 3:13-18
12. John 17:17
13. John 16:13

2 When Your Emotions Are Shut Down

A number of years ago, I was teaching on Luke 9:24, where Jesus declared that those who seek to save their lives will lose them and those who lose their lives for Jesus' sake will find them.

To illustrate the teaching, I came in with about $30 in cash. I intended to pick a person from the class who had a lot of jewelry and possessions with him or her that evening and then "buy" that person's treasures with my money. But before I did this, I first established three things with the class:

1. The things I bought were mine to do with what I pleased. These would be real transactions.
2. The person I picked would have to trust me.
3. The person I picked would be richer when he or she sat down than when he or she stood up.

I ended up picking a young lady I knew very well. She had a tender, loving heart and had some very important jewelry with her that night—items that meant a lot to her. I started off telling her that I would buy her family ring for $5.

Without hesitation, she said, "Okay."

We made the transaction, and I reminded her of my three foundations, especially the first one; these transactions were real, and I could do whatever I wanted with my purchases. I bought jewelry and valuable items from her for very little money — $3 to $5 for each item. Every time I made an offer, she responded positively and without hesitation to the deals.

The Lord began to tell me that something was wrong — she was making the trades too easily. At the end of our bartering, I reminded her that I could do with my purchases whatever I wanted, so I gave the items back to her and told her to keep the money as well. The point of the illustrations was that with Jesus, we never lose — we always come away with a gain.

After the meeting, I took along a young woman, and we asked my friend how she had been able to make the transactions with such ease. As we talked, the Lord revealed that she was in a relationship with a man who had been pushing her to have sex with him. She had resisted for a time, but after a while, she had finally given in to his desires. As a result, she had shut down. Whenever it came to losing something of importance, she would simply check out in order to avoid disappointment and turmoil.

I am glad to say that the Lord healed her heart that night, and the last I heard from her, she was happily married — to another man.

God created emotions to be a part of our physical, spiritual, and soulish composition, so if our emotions are not functioning freely in all facets of our being, something is amiss. If I walked up behind my wife and tapped her on the shoulder, she would feel my fingers and respond. But if I firmly tapped her on the shoulder and she did not feel anything, it would be a signal that something was wrong.

There is a certain physical condition in which a person cannot feel pain. People with this condition, especially children, are at a high risk for physical issues because they can break bones, bite off sections of their tongues, have infections, and be unable to sense the trauma in their bodies. In the same way that a physical inability to feel is dangerous, a soulish and spiritual inability to feel is also dangerous. I have observed numerous people through the years who were emotionally shut down. Some would experience difficult events and yet show no sorrow. Others would see the Lord do an amazing miracle, but their praise would seem empty; there was no emotion behind it. I sometimes watch people in church have difficulty expressing their love and affections for the Lord in praise and thanksgiving.

God wants us to be free to express our hearts to Him fully:

> *"Shout joyfully to the Lord, all the earth.*
> *Serve the Lord with gladness;*
> *Come before Him with joyful singing."*
> — Psalm 100:1–2

Some counselors and ministers direct people to shut down their emotions or even pray that the shutting down would occur. Another common phrase is that emotions would be "put in line with God's Word." But the problem is not the emotion itself — the problem comes because we have trouble discerning what is causing the emotion. Remember that an emotion signals an event, so the question should always be, "What is being signaled here?"

When I minister to people who are dealing with something that is keeping them from walking in God's truth, I tell them to allow His peace to be the referee in determining whether or not a particular issue has been dealt with.[1] However, many times after helping them pray through the hindrance, they do not feel peace.

"I don't feel anything," they say.

Feeling the peace of God is different than not feeling anything — that is, feeling nothing is not His peace. If that is the person's answer, the next step is to participate with God in helping release that person's emotions.

The Lord is very tender in these situations. *"A bruised reed He will not break and a dimly burning wick He will not extinguish; He will faithfully bring forth justice"* (Isaiah 42:3). There is nothing more vulnerable than a bruised reed or a candle that is about to go out. Anything with any level of strength, like a running dog or a puff of wind, can destroy both of these

35

things. When our emotions have been shut down, the Lord will work tenderly with us to restore our ability to feel.

Whenever we deal with shut-down emotions, we first need to determine the reason they are shut down. Here are some of the more common causes.

Traditions of Men

> "See to it that no one takes you captive through philosophy and empty deception, according to the tradition of men, according to the elementary principles of the world, rather than according to Christ." — Colossians 2:8

The first way a person's emotions can be shut down is through the traditions of men. Colossians 2:8 reveals that philosophy, empty deception, and traditions can take us captive. In Greek, that word literally means "to rob" — these things can actually rob us of what has been given to us in Christ. The traditions of men are so powerful that Jesus declared they can render the Word of God ineffective.[2]

Technically speaking, the traditions of men create areas of doubt in our hearts. Our hearts contain our "programming" — our conclusions about life, and those conclusions dictate what we see, hear, speak, feel, do, believe, and even how we love. The person who doubts cannot receive anything from the Lord.[3] When our hearts receive (believe and accept) a religious tradition that is contrary to God's Word, the tradition creates doubt in our hearts and, therefore, shuts us down in that area.

One tradition of men that shuts down emotions is the verbal or nonverbal declaration that emotional expressions, or paying attention to your emotions, is not of God. We know these kinds of declarations are simply a tradition because we have seen that Jesus was a very emotional Person. Throughout Scripture, we read about emotions that can be from the Lord (for example: Psalm 16:11 and 126:1–6). When a religious teaching does not align with the Word of God, it is a tradition or an elementary principle of the world.[4] If we are not careful, these traditions could shut down the emotions God has given us to monitor our lives.

I once ministered to a woman who was struggling with an inability to respond spiritually to the Lord and His gifts. She had been raised in an ultra-traditional liturgical church where emotions could not ever be expressed during a service. As a little girl, she would literally sit in fear of moving during a service. She had not felt the freedom to sneeze or cough. As a result, she was completely shut down emotionally concerning the things of the Spirit.

After the cause of her problem was brought to light, we partnered with the Lord and watched as He beautifully healed her heart of the traditions that were holding her captive. She was freed to flow in the gifts of the Holy Spirit.

How to Find Freedom from Traditions of Men

If a tradition is shutting your emotions down, here are a few steps that can set you free to feel:

1. Forgive whoever communicated the tradition to you.
2. If you have embraced the tradition, ask the Lord to forgive you for your unbelief (for holding to a tradition instead of His truth).
3. "Loosen"[7] your heart from the lie that emotions are not from the Lord.
4. Confess the truth that it is God's will for you to express and experience emotions. The following passages of Scripture are a good support for that truth:

"You will make known to me the path of life;
In Your presence is fullness of joy;
In Your right hand there are pleasures forever."
— Psalm 16:11

"For You make him most blessed forever;
You make him joyful with gladness in Your presence."
— Psalm 21:6

"Then our mouth was filled with laughter
And our tongue with joyful shouting;
Then they said among the nations,
'The Lord has done great things for them.'"
— Psalm 126:2

"Those who sow in tears shall reap with joyful shouting."
— Psalm 126:5

5. Ask the Lord to awaken your soul and spirit to feel the things He created and purposed you to feel.

God created our hearts to feel, and we can't allow the traditions of men to steal the gift of emotions.

Lack of Knowledge

Both Isaiah 5:13 and Hosea 4:6 tell us what can happen when we do not know God's truth:

"Therefore My people go into exile for their lack of knowledge."
— Isaiah 5:13

"My people are destroyed for lack of knowledge. Because you have rejected knowledge, I also will reject you from being My priest. Since you have forgotten the law of your God, I also will forget your children."
— Hosea 4:6

The Isaiah passage reveals that a lack of knowledge is an open door for captivity. If we do not know the truth about emotions, there is a strong possibility that we will not have the freedom to feel—we will be held captive by our lack of understanding.

The Hosea passage takes it one step further when it tells us that we can actually perish because of a lack of knowledge. If a man does not understand that the severe pain in his leg means his leg is broken and so he keeps trying to walk on the leg, the results could be serious. He could even eventually lose that leg. In a similar way, if we do not understand that we are made to feel, we could lose the ability to feel.

I once heard Peter Lord talk about the need to respond to revelations of God's truth. He taught that if we respond to impressions of the Lord, we become more impressionable. Said another way, when we give expression to an impression, we become more impressionable. But when we have impressions and do not express them, our minds will start to block out those impressions. If we don't understand the legitimacy of giving expression to an emotion, that emotion can be shut down.

I was raised in a religious tradition that discouraged every type of emotional expression. In fact, no one in my family had any revelation about emotions and their functions. I watched my mother suffer from a form of depression because she was unable to properly express what she was feeling. She sedated or "stuffed" her emotions. My mother was a precious woman of God. I am a believer in Jesus because of her prayers, but to this day, I believe her lack of knowledge concerning emotions held her captive for many years.

How to Find Freedom from a Lack of Knowledge

1. Make sure you are not harboring unforgiveness toward those who failed to teach you about emotions.
2. Ask the Lord to reveal the truth about your emotions.
3. Ask Him to bring life to your emotions that were shut down.

Traumatic Events

If a person has been raped, abused, or has experienced some type of trauma regarding a friend or loved one, the emotions can be so great that the person shuts them down in order to stay in control of his or her life. We could say the person has experienced a type of psychological, emotional shock.

A similar type of emotion-stuffing traumatic event occurs when a person expresses an emotion and is strongly criticized, made fun of, or condemned for it.

Part of the redemption that Jesus won for us on the cross was to take the pain of emotional sorrows: *"Surely our griefs He Himself bore, and our sorrows He carried; yet we ourselves esteemed Him stricken, smitten of God, and afflicted"* (Isaiah 53:4). The Hebrew word for sorrows can also mean "mental anguish." In other words, on the cross, Jesus carried the mental anguish of our traumatic events. He suffered so our hearts could be emotionally free.

One day as I was closing a campus meeting in prayer, a young man came up behind me and put his arms around me. He was sobbing intensely. I recognized him as a guy who had been in a motorcycle gang before he had joined our group, and I asked some other men to help me pray for him.

When he had calmed down, he began to tell us that he lived in fear of someone coming and attacking him in his sleep. He could not fall asleep at night without knowing his bedroom door was locked. When he was little, his parents divorced, and the man who moved in with his mother abused him. He would yank him out of bed and lock him in dark closets. He would hang the boy upside down and beat him.

As we prayed for this young man, he had a vision of being beaten by his mother's boyfriend, but as the beating occurred, Jesus came, pushed him aside, and took the beating for him. Through this vision, the young man was freed of the emotional pain he had been carrying for years. Jesus literally took the man's pain to the cross.

When a traumatic event occurs in a person's life, the last thing he or she needs is ministry regarding emotions. The most powerful thing we can do is simply be there for that person. It is not a time for theological discussions; it is time for the Body of Christ to be the Body of Christ. *"If one member suffers, all the members suffer with it; if one member is honored, all the members rejoice with it"* (1 Corinthians 12:26).

When I have experienced traumatic events, some of the most powerful moments of comfort involved a brother or sister just crying with me. My son, Shea, was sick as a baby and had to be hospitalized. A precious sister called us to check on him. When I told her what had happened, she cried with me over the phone. That act of compassion still touches my heart when I think about it. Another time, I was hurting, and a brother came to visit me at my home. When I opened the door to let him in, he did not say a word. He simply grabbed me and hugged me and communicated his love for me. I cried like a baby. In both of those situations, my heart was deeply touched and comforted just by the other person being there for me.

In rare and special circumstances when emotions are overwhelmingly intense, a physician's medicinal assistance could help moderate those emotions to a bearable level. As Proverbs 31:6 says, *"Give strong drink to him who is perishing, and wine to him whose life is bitter."* This is only a short-term solution, however; serious addiction issues could arise if certain medications are used for a prolonged period. Under supervision, some medications can help calm a person until their emotions reach equilibrium.

How to Find Freedom from Certain Traumatic Events

I must be careful not to oversimplify the process of healing from traumatic events. Whether the event is the death of a loved one, a rape, some type of ritual abuse, a car wreck, or the effects of war, each type of traumatic event has a path of ministry that can lead to complete emotional healing. Although each path of ministry may differ, restoring emotions that have been shut down from traumatic events usually involves the following steps in some manner:

1. Forgive the people who hurt you or hurt your loved ones.
2. Pray and release your sorrows to the cross of Jesus Christ. Just as He carried your sins and sicknesses, so He wants to carry your sorrows.
3. You may also want to seek God's forgiveness for shutting down emotionally. Renounce the lie that your emotional expression was "bad."
4. Ask the Lord to bring life to your emotions that were shut down.

Overabundance of Emotions

We tend to shut down our emotions when we experience many different emotions at the same time. In this kind of situation, the difficulty lies not with the intensity of the emotion, as it often does with a traumatic event, but there are so many emotions that we cannot process them.

Many prophetic people experience this in a super-charged spiritual environment. If the person does not know how to handle the event or is not under the covering of authority, he or she could easily shut down. One of the purposes of authority is to protect, and concerning emotions, an authority protects by helping us process what we are sensing. Very often, prophetic people in our church will "sound out" with me the things they are feeling. That interaction can release the Lord's wisdom into the situation and bring peace. An authority should also protect through prayer and intercession, making sure that the enemy does not emotionally overwhelm those with prophetic gifting.

I believe an overabundance of emotions was what occurred with Elijah when he shut down emotionally in 1 Kings 19. He had just experienced a series of huge emotional events. He had confronted and killed four hundred prophets of Baal, and then he was spiritually attacked and physically threatened by Jezebel. After these things, the mighty Elijah dropped into a state of fear. He felt alone because he thought he was the only prophet who was still standing for truth. He felt like a failure. He was physically exhausted and hungry.

Emotionally overwhelmed, he asked the Lord to take his life:

> *"But he himself went a day's journey into the wilderness, and came and sat down under a juniper tree; and he requested for himself that he might die, and said, 'It is enough; now, O Lord, take my life, for I am not better than my fathers.'"* — 1 Kings 19:4

Monday mornings are one of the toughest and most vulnerable times for church leaders who preached on Sunday. On Sunday, they gave all they had in ministering the Word of God and participating in the Holy Spirit's ministry, but then on Monday morning, they sometimes receive critical feedback. Because they are already vulnerable, the critical feedback can easily create negative soulish emotions, potentially causing the leaders to shut down.

How to Find Freedom
from an Overabundance of Emotions

1. When you are overwhelmed and your emotions are shutting down, one of the best things you can do is what Elijah did — rest in the Lord and be refreshed in His presence, so you can hear Him in quietness.[5]
2. Seek revelation from God concerning the things you are feeling.
3. Respond to the emotional signals that are important and purposefully lay aside the signals that do not need immediate attention.

4. Make sure you do not have any judgments or unforgiveness issues that need to be dealt with, especially in areas of abandonment or loneliness.

Key Points of Chapter 2

Common Reasons Emotions Can Be Shut Down:

1. Traditions of men
2. Lack of knowledge
3. Traumatic events
4. Overabundance of emotions

Being unable to feel is contrary to God's intended purpose for us. He created us to train our senses to discern good from evil.[6] Whenever we cannot feel, we are vulnerable in that particular area of our lives. God wants to heal and restore to us our ability to feel and discern.

Whatever the reason we have shut down emotionally, the Lord can help us begin to feel again. He will reveal His truth about emotions if we ask Him to do so, but we must partner with Him and allow our emotions to be awakened and released. I often see people refuse to take this journey because of the fear of feeling, but anything the Lord gives is good — He would not lead us into something harmful. We can trust Him with our emotions.

In the next three sections of this book, we will take a detailed look at the three types of emotions (physical, spiritual, and soulish) and how God intended for them to be used in our daily lives.

Notes / Reference Scriptures

1. Colossians 3:15
2. Mark 7:13
3. James 1:6-7; Mark 11:23-24
4. Colossians 2:20-23
5. Isaiah 30:15
6. Hebrews 5:14
7. Matthew 18:18

PART TWO

What Are Physical Emotions?

"Is anyone among you sick? Then he must call for the elders of the church and they are to pray over him, anointing him with oil in the name of the Lord."

— James 5:14

"Blessed be the God and Father of our Lord Jesus Christ, the Father of mercies and God of all comfort, who comforts us in all our affliction so that we will be able to comfort those who are in any affliction with the comfort with which we ourselves are comforted by God."

— 2 Corinthians 1:3-4

Physical emotions are a God-given gift to help us take care of our physical bodies and enjoy the world around us.

We experience physical emotions as a result of the events occurring in or with our bodies. Physical emotions will attempt to direct the flow of our thoughts, but we do not have to allow those emotionally charged thoughts to form conclusions in our hearts that are contrary to God's truth.

3 An Introduction to Physical Emotions

"But his body pains him,
And he mourns only for himself."

— Job 14:22

When I first got married, I was filled with dumbness. I didn't understand the beautiful intricacies of how God had created my wife, Paula. I grew up with a brother, so I knew only "boy stuff." One of the things I definitely did not understand was the female monthly cycle. Paula had notoriously extreme periods. Once a month, she would say things and do things and feel things that did not match who she was the rest of the time. In the beginning, I thought she just needed to get a grip on what she was feeling. There were even times when I wondered if she needed some serious prayer! Needless to say, my lack of understanding caused numerous frustrations in our relationship.

Gradually, I began to realize that the emotions Paula was feeling were not in her mind, nor were they spiritual. She was feeling physical emotions. God created the human body to sense what affects it—that is, the events happening within it. Physical emotions are a fact of life.

As a reminder, when I talk about physical emotions, I mean any sort of feeling that is experienced in the human body. It could be a physical pain, such as what we feel when we step on a tack or get something in our eyes. It could also be a physical emotion like depression, which can be caused by a chemical imbalance. A ride on a roller coaster generates physical emotions, as do the stimulating sounds of music. We have all endured the physical feelings of sickness, injury, hunger, thirst, and weariness.

Physical emotions are a God-created gift that enables us to sense what is happening within and outside our bodies. The main difference between physical emotions and soulish or spiritual emotions is their origin. In most cases, physical emotions begin from some type of stimulus in the physical realm. That stimulus can come from within our bodies (a headache, for example) or from something affecting our bodies externally (such as a car accident).

Interestingly enough, the stimulus can also come from the soul or spirit, which we will examine in a moment.

Types of Physical Emotions

It is important to have a basic understanding of physical emotions so we don't create problems for ourselves or those we love. As we seek to minister to others, we must address their physiological needs as well as their spiritual and soulish needs; otherwise, we could find ourselves chasing proverbial rabbits or causing psychological or spiritual damage.[1]

Physical emotions range from happiness to depression, excitement to weariness, from feeling energetic to feeling sick. In most cases, emotions in our bodies are a result of one of the following five physical occurrences.

Emotions of Physical Need

The body uses physical emotions to signal to the soul that it is in some type of need. Have you ever been exhausted to the point where you no longer acted like yourself? If we're unable to sleep for multiple nights in a row, we could experience emotions that are unstable enough to mirror types of demonic attack. Likewise, if our sugar or potassium levels are out of line, we could have all kinds of strange feelings, visions, and paranoia. A physical need causes a physical emotion, which signals the need.

Emotions of Physical Malfunction

Physical emotions can also arise from a physical malfunction like a sickness, injury, or chemical imbalance. We see this type of emotion described in the Book of Job:

> *"But his body pains him,*
> *And he mourns only for himself." —* Job 14:22

Even though his sickness might have started in the spiritual realm, when Job spoke these words, he was responding to a physical malady or sickness. When we are dealing with an infection, disease, or injury, we can experience a wide variety of emotions. Have you ever severely strained a muscle or torn a ligament? Have you ever needed surgery or suffered from an ulcer? Physical pain can dominate a person's being. The emotions of the body can be significant enough to keep us from feeling the emotions of the soul and spirit.

Emotions of Physical Process

"To the woman He said,
'I will greatly multiply Your pain in childbirth,
In pain you will bring forth children.'"
— Genesis 3:16

A physical process is something the body does naturally. These processes usually include physical emotions; one strong example of this is childbirth.

God created a certain level of feeling to be associated with bringing a child into the world. I believe His original intention was that a woman's physical emotions during the childbirth process would help her prepare for and understand what was happening in her body. When Adam and Eve sinned, it opened the door for that process to become much more painful. Personally, I think God's statement in Genesis 3:16 includes the full process of childbirth—from PMS to the possibility of post-partum depression. Obviously, the childbirth process itself is not a negative process; the potential for increased pain and additional problems came with the introduction of sin.

Emotions of Physical Stimulus

"How beautiful is your love, my sister, my bride!
How much better is your love than wine,
And the fragrance of your oils
Than all kinds of spices!
Your lips, my bride, drip honey;
Honey and milk are under your tongue,
And the fragrance of your garments is like
the fragrance of Lebanon."
— Song of Solomon 4:10–11

Physical emotions can result from a physiological stimulus like touch, sound, or smell. Physical affection shared between a man and a woman, parents and children can make them feel cherished, accepted, and safe.

As I mentioned at the beginning of the chapter, certain sounds can also have a dramatic effect on the human body. Music, for instance, can soothe or calm a person's soul.[2] The sound of drums or a trumpet can excite and inspire an army in battle.[3] Small infants may not be able to understand the parent's words, but the sound of the parent's voice can produce a variety of emotional responses.

The sense of smell is one of the strongest imprinters of information on the heart and mind. To this day, the smell of cut flowers brings back memories of funerals I have attended through the years. We can begin to feel a certain way based on what we smell in the air.

Emotions of Soulish and Spiritual Events

The soul and spirit can cause physical emotions as well. If we see and recognize danger, our minds (the soul) will send signals to our bodies concerning that danger. Our bodies will start to release enzymes into our blood streams, which causes us to experience corresponding physical emotions.

When Jeremiah lost hope in his soul, his physical body started to experience a form of weakness. This physical weakness originated out of the weakness in his soul:

> *"My soul has been rejected from peace;*
> *I have forgotten happiness.*
> *So I say, 'My strength has perished,*
> *And so has my hope from the Lord.'"*
> — Lamentations 3:17–18

Similarly, when we experience spiritual oppression, our physical bodies feel the effects of demonic spirits that have come against us. In Luke 13, Jesus ministered to a woman who had physical pain caused by a demonic spirit: *"There was a woman who for eighteen years had had a sickness caused by a spirit; and she was bent double, and could not straighten up at all"* (verse 11). When Jesus saw her, He called her over to Him, laid His hands on her, and healed her. Immediately she could stand straight and began worshiping God (verse 13).

How Do We Respond to Physical Emotions?

When dealing with physical emotions, it is very important to remember the two basic questions from Chapter 1: What is the emotion signaling? and How do I respond to the signal? Once we know what is causing the physical emotion, the next important step is our response. Some of us have been taught to ignore our physical emotions or "press through." Some of us think we should always act on their promptings. The truth actually lands somewhere in the middle.

Anytime we experience a physical emotion, we should give heed to the emotion. However, we should try not to allow the physical emotion to drive, or force, the direction of our conscious thoughts, nor should we allow the physical emotion to push us into making a conclusion based solely on what we are feeling. Instead, we need to heed the origin of the physical emotion and, if necessary, take appropriate action. There are three steps to responding well to a physical emotion.

Acknowledge the Signal

The first step in dealing with a physical emotion is to acknowledge what we are feeling. Imagine the extensive damage we would do to ourselves if God had not created us to feel pain! In Chapter 1, I talked about putting my hand on a hot stovetop. If I did not acknowledge that pain, I would eventually lose my hand. But after I acknowledge what I am feeling, all I need to do is move my hand from the stove. When we feel some type of physical pain, we need to heed the pain and discover its source.

In ministry, this first step is very important. James 2:15–16 tells us we accomplish nothing when we ignore a person's physical emotions that are arising out of need. When Timothy was having some physical problems, Paul did not tell him to put on a brave face and ignore them. Instead, he acknowledged Timothy's stomach pain and suggested a remedy.[4] We need to acknowledge the feeling and determine its source. Is this emotion coming from my actions or from my lack of action? Is it based within me (in my body, soul, or spirit), or is it coming from an outside source?

The beginning step in dealing with physical emotions is to acknowledge the feeling, which then allows us to determine the source.

Take Appropriate Action

"Is anyone among you sick? Then he must call for the elders of the church and they are to pray over him, anointing him with oil in the name of the Lord."

— James 5:14

After we have determined the source of the physical emotion, we need to take appropriate action, if the situation warrants it. If I were touching a burning object, the appropriate action would be to remove my hand from that object. After Paul acknowledged Timothy's stomach problems, he told him what to do about it — he should use the medicine of their day, which was wine. James tells us that when someone is dealing with physical pain, the appropriate action is for the elders of the church to anoint that person with oil and pray for him or her.

Sometimes, we might have a physical emotion we should not respond to. For example, when a person is coming off of a substance addiction, there will be times when that person's physical body will beg for that substance in various ways, but it is important for that person not to act on those physical emotions.

Discernment is always the key to determining if any action is needed. We look at the truth of God's Word and use the Holy Spirit's emotions (the fruit of the Spirit) to monitor our reception and application of His truth.

Aligned with God's Word

We will have thoughts and emotions based on what our bodies are feeling, but again, we must make every effort to direct the flow of our thoughts and not allow emotionally charged thoughts to form conclusions that are contrary to God's truth. The flow of our spiritual and mental well-being can't be determined by how we feel physically. Our physical emotions change with the events occurring in and around our bodies. Different physical events can cause different physical emotions. If we allow our physical emotions to direct the flow of our thoughts, the content of our thought lives will be unstable. Instead, our spiritual and mental well-being must be established on God's truth.

We can only attempt to direct our thoughts because in certain cases, it simply isn't possible. People who are experiencing physiological forms of mental illness may not be able to direct the flow of their thoughts, which is why God has given us medical professionals who can help us in these kinds of conditions. When these conditions occur, it is not a time for condemnation — it is a time for a sincere cry for help. A person who is struggling with chemically induced depression could have a very difficult time adjusting the flow of his or her thoughts. So whenever possible, it is best to direct our thoughts toward the Lord and the truth of His Word.

When Paula and I were going through childbirth classes, the instructors taught the expectant mothers to focus their thoughts toward a source of comfort. Isaiah 26:3 tells us that we can experience peace through the focus of our thoughts: *"The steadfast of mind You will keep in perfect peace, because he trusts in You."* In Hebrew, trust is the word batach, which can be interpreted as "to attach oneself to." When our minds are "attached to" the goodness of the Lord, we will have peace.

When he penned Psalm 31, David was in pain, yet in the midst of that pain, he chose to direct his thoughts to the Lord:

> *"Be gracious to me, O Lord, for I am in distress;*
> *My eye is wasted away from grief,*
> *my soul and my body also.*
> *For my life is spent with sorrow*
> *And my years with sighing;*
> *My strength has failed because of my iniquity,*
> *And my body has wasted away . . .*
> *But as for me, I trust in You, O Lord,*
> *I say, 'You are my God.'*
> *My times are in Your hand."*
> — Psalm 31:9–10, 14–15

Prayer is one of the tools the Lord has given us so we may supernaturally focus our thoughts on Him, releasing His peace into our hearts and minds.[5] When we do not direct our thoughts, our thoughts can easily be misdirected toward obsessions or sinful actions. Hunger is a positive physical feeling; without it, we would not know when our bodies needed nourishment. But the feeling of hunger could be misdirected into obsessive or sinful actions. When Esau was hungry, he allowed that feeling to cause his thoughts to run rampant. His thoughts then pushed him to take actions he would later regret: He sold his birthright to his brother for some bread and lentil stew.[6]

In an intense time when Jesus experienced the physical emotion of hunger, He did not deny He was hungry; instead, He directed His thoughts, words, and actions toward His Father.[7] He quoted Deuteronomy 8:3: *"Man does not live by bread alone, but man lives by everything that proceeds out of the mouth of the Lord."*

Paul tells us to subject our bodies to our souls: *"I discipline my body and make it my slave, so that, after I have preached to others, I myself will not be disqualified"* (1 Corinthians 9:27; see Romans 6:12 as well). We subject our bodies to our souls so the emotions that are out of line with God's truth may not result in lethal conclusions or actions. We should not allow the emotions of our bodies to compel us toward acts of anger, impatience, frustration, or lust. Touch can generate physical emotions, and inappropriate touch can be deadly.[8] As we grow up physically and spiritually, it is important for us to recognize harmful misuses of physical emotion so we do not fall into sin and become bound by them.

In the few situations in which physical emotions will uncontrollably affect our thinking, professional help should be employed. However, as a whole, we don't have to allow physical emotions to force the direction of our conscious thoughts. Instead, our thoughts need to be continuously in line with God's truth.

Emotions Shouldn't Form Conclusions

Like the sense of smell, emotions are one of the biggest imprinters of information on our hearts. That is one of their most dangerous facets — the information couched inside an emotion will be strongly embedded within us and used to form conclusions.

If you asked most Americans what we were doing on August 11, 2001, I doubt very many of us, if any, would be able to answer with certainty. But if you asked us where we were on September 11, 2001, most of us probably would be able to answer with some detail. The emotion of the memory is the reason for the memory. When we experience physical emotions, Satan often seeks to take advantage of the situation to form conclusions in our hearts. If we allow conclusions that are lies from the enemy to form within us, we could end up experiencing heartache.[9]

Enduring the physical emotions of her menstrual cycle, a woman could easily be pushed to entertain lies that she is overweight, unattractive, or a failure. These conclusions block her from God's truth. Those thoughts are not who she is, but if she entertains these lies, she will not be able to see the truth; the physical emotions she is experiencing can lead her to form false conclusions about herself. To give another example, I know active people who experienced physically debilitating injuries, and in the pain of those injuries, they allowed conclusions of failure to be formed in their hearts. Subsequently, they fell into soulish depression, and in some cases, they even began to entertain thoughts of suicide.

Any time the devil can take advantage of an emotional situation, whether that emotion is positive or painful, he will attempt to do so. He works to establish strongholds of false conclusions in our hearts.[10] A "stronghold" is a military term used to describe an entrenchment or fortification for soldiers. David referred to God as His stronghold,[11] but more often than not, the term stronghold is used to describe one of the ways the enemy works to hinder us. A stronghold of false conclusions can block us off from God's presence, provisions, and truth. When we are blocked off from God in a certain area, we are left open to the enemy's attacks in that area.[A]

Sex is an emotional pleasure that God gave a man and woman to enjoy within the context of marriage.[12] Satan works to take something good like sex and push men and women into perverse and distorted sexual acts, relationships, and addictions. In a similar way, medicinal chemical substances are a part of creation to help in times of sickness or injury. The emotions generated by the substance provide an artificial form of sedation and escape from life's problems; however, any escape that is not Jesus will always have an unhealthy hook to it — a form of death, which the devil uses to enslave people.

When physical emotions occur, we should determine their origin and not allow them to establish an unhealthy pattern of thinking or untrue conclusions in our hearts.

Extreme Physical Malfunctions

What I call extreme physical malfunctions are the feelings we experience when dealing with a serious sickness, injury, or physical disorder. In these situations, it is vital we understand what is happening and how to respond.

I break down this topic into two sections. The first deals with the intense emotions we can physically experience within our own bodies. The second addresses situations in which someone else is experiencing these emotions. Whenever extreme physical emotions are involved, we must use discernment, and our response demands wisdom and understanding.

Facing Our Own Extreme Physical Emotions

*"Beloved, if our heart does not condemn us,
we have confidence before God."* — 1 John 3:21

When we are facing the intense emotions of a major physical malfunction, the pain and confusion can be almost unbearable. I remember times when I was very sick and struggled with the temptation to torment myself with questions: What did I do to release this sickness in my body? Am I doing something wrong? But I have learned that the Lord is more concerned about my welfare than I am. When I rest in His love—and in His willingness and ability to communicate with me anything I need to know—there is not a sense of torment but comfort.

The Lord's presence is our ideal place of comfort, but we won't be able to draw near to Him if we have embraced condemnation in response to the physical issues we are experiencing. When struggling with severe physical emotions, we shouldn't condemn ourselves or even start to pick ourselves apart. Instead, it is time to rest in the love, comfort, and healing of God:

*"You are my hiding place; You preserve me from trouble;
You surround me with songs of deliverance."*
— Psalm 32:7

*"For in the day of trouble He will conceal me in His tabernacle; In the secret place of His tent He will hide me;
He will lift me up on a rock."*
— Psalm 27:5

As I mentioned before, God's Word provides a scriptural basis for the use of medication to give temporary relief from the trauma of extreme physical emotions.[13] Narcotics should be used with wisdom, knowledge, and the good counsel of trained medical professionals. It is possible for medicine to become our confidence and the focus of our faith, rather than the Lord.[14] Obviously, I am not advocating that anyone disobey a doctor's orders, but we don't have to end up using a crutch when, in certain cases, spiritual and mental health could be developed instead.

God is with us to pour His love and power into our hearts, minds, and bodies. His healing and comfort are what we need to remember and cling to when we are experiencing emotions caused by extreme physical malfunctions.

Facing Another's Extreme Physical Emotions

When a loved one is experiencing emotions from an extreme physical malfunction, the most important posture for us is one of comfort:

*"But God, who comforts the depressed,
comforted us by the coming of Titus."*
— 2 Corinthians 7:6

"Blessed be the God and Father of our Lord Jesus Christ, the Father of mercies and God of all comfort, who comforts us in all our affliction so that we will be able to com-

fort those who are in any affliction with the comfort with which we ourselves are comforted by God."
— 2 Corinthians 1:3–4

Remember that comfort is from the Greek word paraklesis, which literally means "to call alongside." I used to think comfort meant the alleviation of discomfort, but I have since discovered that comfort begins when someone comes alongside someone else in order to support that person.

That is not what Job's friends did in his story. His friends were there to critique his life, not stand alongside him in a place of support and intercession. Intercession is an important part of standing alongside a person who is intensely confused or hurting. As we come before God in prayer for our friend, we can trust Him for His relief of the physical emotion, as well as the person's complete healing.

Key Points of Chapter 3

God created the human body to sense what affects it—the events happening within it. Physical emotions are a fact of life. We will have thoughts and emotions based on what our bodies are feeling—but we can control the conclusions we come to.

In the few situations in which physical emotions will uncontrollably affect our thinking, professional help should be employed. However, as a whole, we shouldn't allow physical emotions to force the direction of our conscious thoughts. Instead, our thoughts need to be continuously in line with God's truth.

How Do We Deal with Physical Emotions?

1. We should acknowledge the feeling, which allows us to determine its source.
2. After we have determined the emotion's source, we need to take appropriate action, if the situation warrants it. Discernment is always the key to determining if any action is needed.

When physical emotions occur, we can determine their origin and not allow them to establish an unhealthy pattern of thinking, or untrue conclusions, in our hearts.

Notes / Reference Scriptures

[A] For more information about strongholds, visit www.dealingjesus.org

1. James 2:15-16
2. 1 Samuel 16:16
3. Joshua 6:5
4. 1 Timothy 5:23
5. Philippians 4:6-8
6. Genesis 25:29-34
7. Matthew 4:2-4
8. 1 Peter 2:11; Romans 8:6
9. John 8:44
10. 2 Corinthians 10:3-5
11. 2 Samuel 22:3
12. Proverbs 5:18-19
13. Proverbs 31:6; 1 Timothy 5:23
14. Romans 14:23; 2 Chronicles 16:12

PART THREE

What Are Soulish Emotions?

"Peace I leave with you; My peace I give to you; not as the world gives do I give to you. Do not let your heart be troubled, nor let it be fearful."

— John 14:27

Soulish emotions alert us to what is happening in our souls. They show us what we believe to be true or to be false. We can control our soulish emotions when we control the focus of our minds and the conclusions of our hearts.

4 An Introduction to Soulish Emotions

For a time, I struggled with depression. I had made some mistakes in ministry, and as a result, I became overwhelmed by feelings of failure and hopelessness. Things got so intense at one point that I was seriously considering taking my life. I did not completely realize why and what I was feeling, even though I had experience in this area; I had ministered the Lord's freedom to people who were going through all kinds of fears and depressions.

This period of time climaxed one day when I was sitting alone up in the Virginia mountains. I said to myself, "I could not be trusted with the ministries the Lord has and would give to me. The Lord has forgotten me and the Lord has forsaken me!" Those thoughts bounced around in my head like a golf ball in a metal bucket. The more I contemplated them, the more hopeless I felt, like an absolute failure.

I decided I was going to open my Bible at random and just see what the Lord would say to me. My Bible fell open to Isaiah 49:14: *"But Zion said, 'The Lord has forsaken me, and the Lord has forgotten me.'"* When I read that, I said, "There it is in black and white — the Lord has forgotten me and the Lord has forsaken me!"

But the Lord gently said to me, "Read the rest of the passage."

I began to do so:

> *"Can a woman forget her nursing child*
> *And have no compassion on the son of her womb?*
> *Even these may forget, but I will not forget you.*
> *"Behold, I have inscribed you on the palms of My hands;*
> *Your walls are continually before Me."*
>
> — Isaiah 49:15–16

As I completed the passage, joy and peace began to fill my soul. I wrote my name on my hand so the next time the soulish emotions of depression tried to fill me, I could hold my hand up to my face and say, "The Lord will not forget me. He has written my name on His hand." I began to saturate myself with God's lovingkindness and faithfulness. The "facts" of my life, not the truth, had been filling me, so I was haunted by the soulish emotions of depression and failure. As God's truth sank into my heart, my soulish emotions changed, and hope filled me instead. Joy and expectations of a positive future signaled my reception of His truth in my soul.

Contrary to popular belief, the ability to feel depression is not a bad thing. The bad thing is the lie, or lies, being signaled by the feeling of depression. If I did not have the ability to feel the lies, I would never know they were inside my soul, and therefore, I would not realize something needed to change within me.

Think about it this way: If I have strep throat, I want to know about it, so I can deal with it and keep it from potentially causing more serious problems in my body. The pain in my throat tells me of the problem. The pain is not the problem — the infection is the problem. Cure the infection, and the pain will go away. The pain in the throat is how we know whether or not the infection has been eradicated. The feeling of depression does the same thing; it alerts me to the presence of a problem. When the soulish depression is gone, it is a signal to me that the false conclusion has been dealt with. So many times people get frustrated with what they are feeling, and they try to get rid of the emotion, thinking the emotion is the problem. We must train ourselves to respond to the source of the emotion, not just the emotion itself.

This book defines emotions as a signal of an event. Just as physical emotions usually signal an event in the physical realm, soulish emotions typically signal an event in the soul. This is my working definition of soulish emotions:

A soulish emotion is a signal of a mindset, conclusion, or stored emotion in the heart.

Soulish emotions occur when we encounter an environment that exposes our beliefs. When Jesus broke the news to His disciples that He was about to leave them, the soulish emotion of sorrow started filling their minds and hearts:

> *"But because I have said these things to you, sorrow has filled your heart."*   — John 16:6

We can see the conclusion, or belief, that was being established within them, and it is why Jesus warned them not to let their hearts become troubled.[1] Another example of this is when the disciples realized that demons were subject to them in Jesus' name. They were joyful.[2] This positive emotion of joy signaled a revelation down in their hearts.

Conclusions that are being established in our hearts give off signals—we will be able to feel them. If someone throws me a baseball and I catch it, I can feel the baseball in my glove. The sensation of the ball in my glove signals to me that I caught the ball. When we receive a verbal or nonverbal communication from someone, the feeling signals to us that our hearts have heard the communication. The feeling also signals how our hearts received it.

Origins of Soulish Emotions

Three different sources in our souls can generate soulish emotions. A soulish emotion can come from the current focus of the conscious mind, from a conclusion or belief, or from an emotion of a past event that has been stored in the heart. Let's look at these a little more closely.

Focus of the Conscious Mind

The conscious mind (a part of the soul) determines our source of information. When we focus our conscious minds on the flesh or the world, that mindset will release fleshly emotions within us.[3] When we focus our minds on the things of Heaven and God, our souls will be filled with spiritual emotions.

Conclusions or Beliefs

Soulish emotions can also come from something we believe — that is, from a conclusion in our hearts (the sub-conscious mind). The soul signals the body or draws on the spirit about the perceived event, and the body and spirit respond accordingly.

Example: A man believes rattlesnakes are dangerous. He has no past experience with rattlesnakes, either good or bad, but if he is walking along a trail and sees a rattlesnake, his beliefs and generated thoughts about rattlesnakes will cause his body to respond in fear.

Stored Emotions

Finally, soulish emotions can be the emotions of a past conclusion. Unlike beliefs in the heart, which do not require an actual experience, stored emotions are formed when we experience an event that "marks" us in some way.

Example: After having a traumatic experience with a snake, a man makes a conclusion about that event and stores it in his heart. If he thinks about or sees a snake, that stored conclusion will release the unprocessed emotions of the past, plus any physical emotions generated by the soul as it signals the body about the snake.

In order to understand and use soulish emotions appropriately, we need to understand their significance and how they function.

Soulish Emotions and Timing

Soulish emotions encompass two separate periods of time: the past and the present. We need to differentiate between the two periods because we deal with their emotions in different ways.

With a current event, the heart and mind are interpreting and seeking to cope with a sudden change in the environment. When Jesus told His disciples He was going to leave them, He also told them, "Don't let your heart be troubled." The thought of Jesus' departure filled the disciples' souls with sorrow, and He tried to help them cope with that sorrow. The disciples were dealing with soulish emotions that signaled a current event.

With a stored conclusion from a past event, the mind and heart are re-experiencing and trying to cope with the emotions of the past. Imagine that one of Jesus' disciples had been abandoned as a child. When Jesus told them He was leaving, that disciple's heart and mind would release all of the stored information and emotions from that past abandonment. He would likely think, Here we go again. Or, Why am I always left behind? In that moment, many of his emotions would be emerging from a past event.

Whether the soulish emotion is arising from events of the past or from a stored conclusion that is interpreting the present situation, the emotion does not have to be negative or painful; it can also be a feeling such as happiness and peace. A familiar song from the past can bring up the joyful or peaceful soulish emotions we were storing the first time we heard that song.

The Content of Our Hearts

We control our soulish emotions when we control the beliefs and conclusions of our hearts. Whenever we feel lonely, for example, we are likely dealing with a soulish emotion. Many times we try to deal with the feeling of loneliness and end up in sin or sedating the feeling with drugs or alcohol. However, if we understand the origin of the loneliness, we can take action to alleviate the pressure of the emotion.

> *"Do not let your heart be troubled; believe in God,*
> *believe also in Me."* — John 14:1

In this passage, Jesus warned the disciples about soulish emotions. Notice He told them not to let their hearts feel those emotions. In other words, they were not to allow the beliefs and conclusions of their hearts to be influenced by the world's distractions.

I have counseled many people who were dealing with fear and panic attacks. One of the things I have learned is that you do not tell someone who is about to have a panic attack, "Do not be afraid." Jesus was not saying these things to frustrate the disciples. Instead, He was telling them the key to controlling their current soulish emotions—we control our emotions when we control the beliefs and conclusions of our hearts.

Environments Reveal Our Beliefs

Most of the time, the beliefs and conclusions of the heart lie dormant until an environment causes them to arise in the conscious mind. The Bible refers to this type of environment as a trial or wilderness.

Peter states that trials and environments will prove, or reveal, our beliefs.[4] The Greek word for trial means "to puncture" or "to pass through." Essentially, it means to experience an event or, for our context, to be in an environment that reveals a particular belief. When we go through a trial or wilderness, the pressure of that environment will reveal the beliefs and stored conclusions of our hearts:

> *"You shall remember all the way which the Lord your God has led you in the wilderness these forty years, that He might humble you, testing you, to know what was in your heart, whether you would keep His commandments or not."* — Deuteronomy 8:2

A wilderness is a place of "no props"—that is, everyone or everything on which we normally depend is removed, and the Lord is revealed as our sole Source of nourishment and dependency. If the Lord is not our source of fulfillment, the wilderness will reveal that conclusion of the heart as well.

Environment (trial, wilderness) > Conclusions and Beliefs

73

When I teach on this topic, I will ask someone in the class what his or her conclusions are about rattlesnakes. Usually, that person will tell me that rattlesnakes are dangerous and he or she prefers not to be around rattlesnakes.

I will then ask the person if he or she has any fear of rattlesnakes at that moment. Usually, the answer is "No." However, if I ask that person to imagine that a six-foot rattler is being released right next to the chair, the answer changes! That person will often tell me, "If that happened, I would feel afraid."

That rattlesnake would not have done anything to the person physically or spiritually, but that person would still be afraid. The environment is exposing the person's conclusions about rattlesnakes. The late Steve Irwin, the "Crocodile Hunter," had no such conclusions in his heart about poisonous snakes. If placed in the same environment, he would have had a different response to the rattler because his conclusions were different.

Environments reveal the beliefs and conclusions of our hearts, and it is those beliefs and conclusions that generate soulish emotions.

Exposed Beliefs Generate Thoughts

When an environment exposes our beliefs, our conscious minds begin to fill with thoughts related to those exposed beliefs.

Environment (trial, wilderness) > Conclusions and Beliefs > Thoughts

If I believe rattlesnakes are dangerous and a rattlesnake appears in my environment, my mind will flood with thoughts about the danger of rattlesnakes. Conversely, if I believe rattlesnakes are not dangerous, the thoughts generated out of my beliefs will be positive. I have heard of children who played with snakes as if they were toys because they had no knowledge of the danger. A child's beliefs generate thoughts that do not limit what they can or cannot do. The types of beliefs we have acquired determine the types of thoughts that flow through our conscious minds.

In Luke 8:24–25, Jesus' disciples were emotionally shaken by a fierce storm that started to overwhelm their boat. The environment of the life-threatening storm did not bother Jesus, but the disciples, many of whom were experienced fishermen and had been on the sea countless times, were convinced they were about to drown. The environment of the storm exposed their beliefs about Jesus:

> *"They came to Jesus and woke Him up, saying, 'Master, Master, we are perishing!' And He got up and rebuked the wind and the surging waves, and they stopped, and it became calm. And He said to them, 'Where is your faith?' They were fearful and amazed, saying to one another, 'Who then is this, that He commands even the winds and the water, and they obey Him?'"*

They did not truly know the awesomeness and power of the One who was in the boat with them—they did not understand who Jesus is. When they perceived that their environment was dangerous, their minds filled with thoughts of fear. The same environment for Jesus revealed the security He had as the Son of God; He could sleep in the midst of the storm.

When an environment exposes our beliefs, our beliefs will generate thoughts that will try to fill our conscious minds.

Thoughts Generate Emotions

The beliefs in our hearts generate our thoughts, and our thoughts then generate feelings.

Environment (trial, wilderness) > Conclusions and Beliefs > Thoughts > Emotions

In the Garden of Gethsemane the night before Jesus was crucified, He experienced the trauma of intense soulish emotions. The progression of His soulish emotions occurred when thoughts of bearing the world's sin began to fill His soul. He told His disciples, "My soul is deeply grieved, to the point of death," and verbally expressed to His Father how He felt about drinking the cup of sufferings.[5]

In Romans 9:2–3, Paul revealed a similar inner process. He was thinking about the fate of his fellow countrymen, and those thoughts caused emotions to arise in his heart:

> *"I have great sorrow and unceasing grief in my heart. For I could wish that I myself were accursed, separated from Christ for the sake of my brethren, my kinsmen according to the flesh."*

We feel soulish emotions when our beliefs generate thoughts and our thoughts subsequently generate emotions.

Soulish Emotions Lead to Actions

When they are fully established within us, our emotions will inspire or attempt to push us into some type of action.

Environment (trial, wilderness) > Conclusions and Beliefs > Thoughts > Emotions > Actions

In Numbers 13 and 14, the children of Israel learned that giants lived in the Promised Land, and the thought of facing those giants generated a great deal of fear within them:

> *"'Only do not rebel against the Lord; and do not fear the people of the land, for they will be our prey. Their protection has been removed from them, and the Lord is with us; do not fear them.' But all the congregation said to stone*

them with stones. Then the glory of the Lord appeared in the tent of meeting to all the sons of Israel."

— Numbers 14:9–10

Israel allowed their fear to grow until it pushed them into rebellion and even the desire to murder their leaders. David declares in Psalm 37:8, *"Cease from anger and forsake wrath; do not fret; it leads only to evildoing."* Negative emotions can become so strong and compelling that they eventually drive us to take unwise actions.

On the other end of the spectrum, soulish emotions can also inspire us to take positive actions. Paul's first letter to the Corinthian church revealed the sin in their hearts. In response, they experienced a soulish emotion of sorrow that led to their repentance.[6]

What we believe determines what we think. What we think determines what we feel. What we feel can determine what we do.

Soulish Emotions and Adversities

It is a given that in this world, we will come head to head with adversities. Those adversities include experiences like trials and temptations, tribulations and wildernesses (what some call the dark night of the soul). When we face difficult situations, it is important for us to have good foundations established in our hearts and minds so both are protected from out-of-control soulish emotions. The devil wants rampant soulish emotions to push us into actions that are contrary to God's truth.

In his first letter to the Thessalonian church, Paul warned his readers that adversities could disturb their faith through emotional distress:

> *"We sent Timothy, our brother and God's fellow worker in the gospel of Christ, to strengthen and encourage you as to your faith, so that no one would be disturbed by these afflictions; for you yourselves know that we have been destined for this. For indeed when we were with you, we kept telling you in advance that we were going to suffer affliction; and so it came to pass, as you know."*
> — 1 Thessalonians 3:2–4

The devil uses environments of adversity to pressure our souls in three ways. He designed the storms of life to squeeze us so we lose our hope in the Lord and our focus on the Holy Spirit, which causes us to lose positive spiritual emotions such as peace and joy. That is what Paul was warning the Thessalonians about.

Second, life's storms are designed to release the negative emotions stored in our hearts: anger, hate, fear, striving, impatience, and many others like these. Negative soulish emotions make it difficult for us to hear revelation from the Lord. When we are battling negative soulish emotions, our lives can easily be shaken, which is why the Lord warned Joshua about fear and discouragement in Joshua 1:9.

Finally, the devil hopes to use life's storms to establish new negative conclusions and emotions within us.[7] These emotions are designed by the enemy to carry lies that can negatively affect our faith. When these emotions and the lies they contain take root in our hearts, our faith can easily be shipwrecked. All three of these demonic goals will seek to take captive areas in our souls and cut off our trust in God.

Establishing Foundations of God's Truth

> *"Therefore, let everyone who is godly pray to You in a time when You may be found;*
> *Surely in a flood of great waters they will not reach him."*
> — Psalm 32:6

When I coached football, one of the most crucial things I taught was the importance of being in a ready position. If we are not in a ready position, we can easily be defeated, but if we are in a ready position, we are better able to handle whatever our opponent throws at us. The same is true in everyday life: When dealing with emotions, one of the most important things is being in a ready position.

For years, I lived with an edge of uncertainty toward trials and tribulations. One day, the Lord revealed to me that I was looking for the "happily ever after" part of life. Most of the movies I had seen as a child ended with the main characters living in what seemed to be a permanent state of bliss, and that observation had filtered into my Christian walk. In my own life, it seemed that every time one trial was ending, another was just coming around the corner. Because I was subconsciously looking for the happily ever after, a measure of discouragement anchored in my soul.

As God led me through this discovery process, I realized He never promised us lives of ease. In fact, Jesus even warned us, *"In the world you have tribulation"* (John 16:33). But He also told us that in Him, we can overcome the world and its adversities. Our ability to overcome the world is a direct result of the foundations we establish in our hearts. Like the foundations of a building, the foundations of our hearts keep us steady in the midst of life's storms.[8]

Paul gave an example of these foundations in 1 Thessalonians 4:13: *"But we do not want you to be uninformed, brethren, about those who are asleep, so that you will not grieve as do the rest who have no hope."* The sorrow of death is a tribulation every one of us faces, whether it is the threat of our own death or the death of a loved one. When my mother and brother were dying, the enemy tried to shake my soul with the trauma of watching them suffer. I could actually hear the taunts of sickness and death being spoken into me. But the Lord had laid foundations of truth in my heart that enabled me to stand in victory. When my mother and brother passed away, I was able to deal with my sorrow with a sense of security and hope.

If we have allowed God's truth to be established in our hearts, we will not be rocked by strong emotions during times of trauma. I don't mean to imply that we will not feel strong emotions, but our foundations in God serve as an anchor for our souls; we can face the death of a loved one with a sense of comfort because of His truth.

I have found that in His Word, God often operates with the expectation that we will participate with Him. There are three different ways a Greek verb can relate to a noun. One is active, where the subject does the action. One is passive, where the subject receives the action. The third one, however, is where the subject participates in the action.[9] This subject-verb relationship provides a good word picture concerning our heavenly Father's desire for us to participate with Him.[10] As God reveals truth to us, we participate with Him in the revelation of that truth. The Holy Spirit reveals the truth, but it is our responsibility to:

1. Receive it with an honest and good heart.[11]
2. Hold it fast.
3. Practice it, as James talks about. Be doers of the word. That Greek word literally means "practice," like you would practice shooting a basketball or throwing a football.

When we hear a revelation of God, we should receive it, memorize it, meditate on it, allow the reality of it to be birthed in our hearts, and then practice it in the situations the world gives us as obstacles to God's truth.

Because of the world's uncertainties and pressures, the best time to establish a strong foundation with God is before anything difficult happens. We can gain victory over the storms of life before those storms even start, and then when they come, they will not be able to reach our souls.[12] In the midst of them, we will be able to walk in peace and joy.

Jesus speaks of this incredible state of heart in Matthew 7:24–25:

> *"Therefore everyone who hears these words of Mine and acts on them, may be compared to a wise man who built his house on the rock. And the rain fell, and the floods came, and the winds blew and slammed against that house; and yet it did not fall, for it had been founded on the rock."*

If we lay the foundations of God firmly in our lives, the world's storms cannot shake our souls.

Jesus laid such foundations in the disciples' hearts. He did not want the coming difficulties to destabilize their emotions after He ascended into Heaven. Six times in John 14–16 He used the phrase, *"These things I have spoken to you,"* which was meant to solidify His words in His listeners. Three of those six times Jesus included foundations for soulish emotions:

> *"These things I have spoken to you while abiding with you. But the Helper, the Holy Spirit, whom the Father will send in My name, He will teach you all things, and bring to your remembrance all that I said to you. Peace I leave with you; My peace I give to you; not as the world gives do I give to you. Do not let your heart be troubled, nor let it be fearful."* — John 14:25–27

> *"These things I have spoken to you so that **My joy may be in you**, and that your joy may be made full."* — John 15:11, (emphasis added)

> *"These things I have spoken to you, so that **in Me you** may have peace."* — John 16:33, (emphasis added)

When we establish foundations of truth in our hearts, peace and joy will be ours in abundance, no matter the circumstances we face.

As the Hebrews sought to enter the Promised Land, the missing foundations of truth in their lives became obvious. More than once, they were overtaken by negative emotions that played a significant part in keeping them out of the Promised Land:

> *"Then all the congregation lifted up their voices and cried, and the people wept that night. All the sons of Israel grumbled against Moses and Aaron; and the whole congregation said to them, 'Would that we had died in the land of Egypt! Or would that we had died in this wilderness!'"* — Numbers 14:1–2

However, later under Joshua's leadership, Israel worked with him to establish foundations of truth. God commanded Joshua to guard his soul from negative emotions:

> *"Have I not commanded you? Be strong and courageous! Do not tremble or be dismayed, for the Lord your God is with you wherever you go."* — Joshua 1:9

That foundation of courage and strength enabled Joshua to lead the Hebrews through many obstacles. It will do the same for you.

Key Points of Chapter 4

A soulish emotion is a signal of a mindset, conclusion, or stored emotion in our hearts. The ability to sense soulish emotions is a God-given gift that enables us to know what is occurring in our hearts and minds.

The Key to Controlling Soulish Emotions

We control our emotions when we control the beliefs and conclusions of our hearts. This is how it works:

1. Environments reveal the beliefs and conclusions of our hearts.
2. Our beliefs determine the types of thoughts that flow through our conscious minds.
3. Our thoughts generate our emotions.
4. Our emotions push us into some type of action.

What we believe determines what we think. What we think determines what we feel. What we feel can determine what we do.

What Do the Storms of Life Try to Do?

1. Life's storms squeeze us and try to make us lose our hope in the Lord and our focus on the Holy Spirit, which then causes us to lose positive spiritual emotions such as peace and joy.
2. Life's storms can release the negative emotions stored in our hearts: anger, hate, fear, striving, impatience, and many others like these.
3. Life's storms try to establish new negative conclusions and emotions within us. Designed by the enemy, these emotions carry lies that can negatively affect our faith.

Our ability to overcome the world is a direct result of the foundations we establish in our hearts. Like the foundations of a building, the foundations of our hearts keep us steady in the midst of life's storms. As we establish foundations of truth in our hearts, we will be able to walk in abundant peace and joy.

Notes / Reference Scriptures

1. John 14:1
2. Luke 10:17
3. Romans 8:5-6; Galatians 5:22-23
4. 1 Peter 1:6-7
5. Matthew 26:36-39
6. 2 Corinthians 7:8-10
7. 1 Samuel 30:1-6
8. Psalm 11:3
9. Acts 1:8; Philippians 2:12-13
10. Mark 16:20; 1 Corinthians 3:9; 2 Corinthians 6:1
11. Luke 8:15
12. Psalm 32:6-7

5 Common Soulish Emotions

When I was a kid, I accidentally stepped on a nail. I felt it as soon as it broke my skin, and I was able to lift my foot so the nail did not penetrate it completely. I know that story is a "grimacing" way to begin a chapter, but it has clear similarities with how God created the human heart. He created us in such a way that our hearts can tell when a deadly lie has penetrated them. As we discern the lie, we can appropriately respond and remove it from our hearts.

We can also discern when our hearts are embracing a truth of God. We can then respond to that truth and empower our hearts to become solidified and fortified in Him.

Our hearts and minds were created to be very sensitive to the feeling of thoughts, so it is important we familiarize ourselves with the emotions associated with truth, as well as the emotions associated with lies. There are two important questions I like to pose to people when I am ministering to them:

What does a lie feel like?
What does truth feel like?

The Word of God tells us that a mature man or woman can discern good from evil.[1] One of the applications of that passage is that the mature man or woman can feel the difference between truth and lies.

In Chapter 1, we talked about the two major resources we have to discern our emotions and their sources: the Holy Spirit and the Word of God. The goal is for us to allow the Word of God and the Holy Spirit to help us judge the emotions we are experiencing. God's Word describes the emotions associated with truth and the emotions associated with lies, and the Holy Spirit is the Revealer of truth, the reality of truth, and the feelings of truth described by Scripture. In other words, we can tell the emotions of truth by the feelings of the Holy Spirit.

Remember that when the Holy Spirit reveals something, the fruit of the Spirit will be present: *"The wisdom from above is first pure, then peaceable, gentle, reasonable, full of mercy and good fruits, unwavering, without hypocrisy"* (James 3:17). When the Holy Spirit speaks, we will be able to feel His love, joy, and peace. If we don't feel love, joy, and peace, something is amiss. That is why Paul tells us, *"Let the peace of Christ rule in your hearts, to which indeed you were called in one body; and be thankful"* (Colossians 3:15).

It is important for us to note that the emotions in line with God's truth are spiritual emotions generated by the Holy Spirit. When we are talking about soulish emotions of truth, we are talking about the conclusions of Spirit and truth being established in our hearts.

In this chapter, we are going to discuss a few of the emotions that can be associated with the feelings of lies or the feelings of God's truth.

Soulish Feelings of Failure

Every person on the earth has sensed the feelings of failure in some measure. These feelings were particularly strong for Joshua and the elders of Israel after they were defeated by the tiny nation of Ai. The Hebrew children had just watched God perform a mighty miracle; right in front of them, He had brought down the walls of the seemingly invincible city of Jericho. No doubt, that victory made their unexpected defeat feel all the more horrific and shameful. Joshua 7:6-7 gives us a picture of the emotions that filled Joshua's soul—the same emotions that can fill our souls when we feel defeated:

"Then Joshua tore his clothes and fell to the earth on his face before the ark of the Lord until the evening, both he and the elders of Israel; and they put dust on their heads. Joshua said, 'Alas, O Lord God, why did You ever bring this people over the Jordan, only to deliver us into the hand of the Amorites, to destroy us? If only we had been willing to dwell beyond the Jordan!'"

Joshua and the elders of Israel tore their clothes and fell on the ground. These actions portray thoughts of helplessness, desperation, and hopelessness. When emotions of defeat fill our souls, we often feel totally helpless and unable to complete or accomplish even the smallest task. Desperation and hopelessness are also common symptoms of feeling like a failure.

In Joshua 7, Joshua and the elders cried out to the Lord and even questioned His very character by asking why He would give them over to the Amorites to be destroyed. But God had not brought them out of Egypt to be defeated—He had brought them out so they could enter their Promised Land. When Achan's sin was exposed and dealt with, the Israelites attacked Ai again, this time successfully.

Soulish Feelings of Success

"But thanks be to God, who always leads us in triumph in Christ, and manifests through us the sweet aroma of the knowledge of Him in every place."

— 2 Corinthians 2:14

Conversely, the feelings of success often involve a sense of thankfulness and gratitude. Have you ever seen an athlete or politician give an interview after a victory? A common theme is the expression of gratitude or thanks; they feel successful, and this puts them in a more generous and open mood. As believers in Jesus Christ, we can walk in feelings of success every day because we have a promise from God that He is continually working to bring us into a place of victory.[2] Thanksgiving and gratitude should be second nature to us.

Another outcome of feeling successful is feeling confident. When success is assured, confidence can fill our souls:

> *"For I am confident of this very thing, that He who began a good work in you will perfect it until the day of Christ Jesus."* — Philippians 1:6

> *"By this, love is perfected with us, so that we may have confidence in the day of judgment; because as He is, so also are we in this world."* — 1 John 4:17

When I played sports and my team faced an opponent we knew we overmatched, we felt confident as we walked into the event. Similarly, when our hearts are in love with the Lord, confidence can easily fill us. We have this confidence because we know that He can bring us victoriously into His presence, no matter the obstacles set before us.

Joy is another feeling associated with success. Have you ever watched a movie or read a book that included a victorious battle scene? As the good guys realize they have won, a loud, tangible joy overcomes them. We can face trials and temptations with the soulish emotion of joy because the outcome of adversity is our perfection and completion. On the other side of this trial, we will lack in nothing:

> *"Though you have not seen Him, you love Him, and though you do not see Him now, but believe in Him, you greatly rejoice with joy inexpressible and full of glory, obtaining as the outcome of your faith the salvation of your souls."* — 1 Peter 1:8-9

> *"Consider it all joy, my brethren, when you encounter various trials, knowing that the testing of your faith produces endurance. And let endurance have its perfect result, so that you may be perfect and complete, lacking in nothing."* — James 1:2-4

Any time we do not feel successful, we feel defeated, which means our souls are likely generating thoughts and conclusions of failure. The feelings of failure signal the presence of lies in our hearts and minds regarding our circumstances. The Word of God tells us He always leads us toward victory.[3] Once we know that a lie has been established in our hearts, we can take the appropriate measures to change the conclusion that the emotion of failure is signaling within us.

Soulish Feelings of Anxiety and Worry Versus Peace

Anxiety is a soulish emotion God does not want in the souls of His children — ever.

> *"Be anxious for nothing, but in everything by prayer and supplication with thanksgiving let your requests be made known to God."* — Philippians 4:6

> *"Do not be worried about your life, as to what you will eat or what you will drink; nor for your body, as to what you will put on. Is not life more than food, and the body more than clothing? . . . And who of you by being worried can add a single hour to his life? And why are you worried about clothing? Observe how the lilies of the field grow; they do not toil nor do they spin."*
> — Matthew 6:25, 27-28

Science bears witness to the fact that anxiety and worry are not good for our physical and emotional health. Anxiety can even cause physical infirmities. Anxiety, or worry, is from a family of Greek words that gives us a picture of our thoughts or cares being divided. When we worry, we allow our minds to be divided into many concerns, rather than focusing on the truth that our heavenly Father loves us and wants to take care of us.[4]

Notice in the Matthew passage that Jesus tells us the feelings of worry and anxiety involve "toiling." Toil means "to weary or exhaust oneself." When we are worried, we often feel like we cannot rest or that we have to do something. The main effect of worry, however, is reflected in the term spin. When we worry, our minds spin from thought to thought. The effects of worry are like someone trying to point at a particular object on the wall while spinning in an office chair. As long as that person is "spinning," he or she is unable to point with accuracy. Worry hinders our minds from focusing on the thoughts we should be thinking.

God's antithesis to worry and anxiety is peace. The peace of God is a state of rest, tranquility, and stability for our souls. Peace guards our hearts and minds,[5] and it comes when our thoughts are focused on the Lord's character and provisions.[6] We do not have to endure anxious thoughts—we can fix our minds on the Lord and His loving care for us, and as a result, the peace of God will bring rest and tranquility to our souls.

Soulish Feelings of Hopelessness

"Hope deferred makes the heart sick,
But desire fulfilled is a tree of life."
— Proverbs 13:12

In English, we tend to consider hope as a lesser form of faith, but the reality is that hope is the object or focus of our faith:

"Now faith is the assurance of things hoped for, the conviction of things not seen" (Hebrews 11:1). We believe and trust in the object of our hope. If we have no hope, we have nothing to activate our faith.

Hope is the anchor of our souls.[7] It gives our souls stability, and without hope, our souls can experience a variety of negative emotions. Hopelessness is the root of suicide. When people become hopeless about their lives and opportunities, it is not difficult for the devil to influence them into believing the lie that they should end the pain permanently. When the Amalekites kidnapped the families of David and his mighty men, his men lost hope and sought to kill him. When Peter lost hope, he went back to fishing, instead of seeking to embrace his future in Christ. When Judas was without hope, he hung himself.

Like the men and women of the Bible, most of us will experience the emotions of hopelessness at some point in our lives. The only time in my life I entertained thoughts of suicide was when the mind-numbing feelings of hopelessness had filled me. In the process, I discovered the importance of recognizing what was being signaled within me and then responding appropriately.

The Results of Hopelessness

In Luke 24:13–21, two of Jesus' followers felt hopeless as they traveled the road to Emmaus. Before His crucifixion, these men had been filled with hope and had trusted that Jesus was the One to deliver Israel, but when He died, their expectations were brutally dashed.

The first emotional response of hopelessness is sadness and grief. When a hope is seemingly gone, sorrow fills us. In many cases, we can see how fully our lives were invested in that particular hope based on the extent of our sadness and grief.

The second emotional response that occurs with hopelessness is the inability to see and feel God working in our midst. In Luke 24, the men were unable to recognize the resurrected Jesus, even though He was physically walking with them. They knew Him face to face — but their hearts were broken, and they did not recognize the life being offered to them. I have talked with many people who were dealing with hopelessness, and they kept repeating that the Lord had abandoned them. But that is something God would never do.[8] In the moment, they simply cannot see the life being offered to them.

Another common result of hopelessness is unrestraint. Proverbs 29:18 says, *"Where there is no vision, the people are unrestrained."* Unrestraint doesn't necessarily mean actions of rage or violence; often, it is a what-is-the-use? mentality. When we start operating in an unrestrained manner, we let things go. People with unrestrained hearts do not care how they look or how their houses or rooms are ordered; they do not care about the state of their spiritual lives or their occupations. The unrestrained heart has no hope for the future and therefore lives in a state of unconcern.

How to Respond to Hopelessness

Hopelessness is a serious condition; therefore, it is important for us to be able to identify the symptoms of hopelessness and respond appropriately. I know of four responses that can help us in this time of need. The first is what Jeremiah did when he was experiencing hopelessness in Lamentations 3:

> *"My soul has been rejected from peace;*
> *I have forgotten happiness.*
> *So I say, 'My strength has perished,*
> *And so has my hope from the Lord.'"*
>
> — Lamentations 3:17–18

When he was in a state of total hopelessness, he started calling to mind the nature and character of God:

> "Remember my affliction and my wandering, the worm-
> wood and bitterness.
> Surely my soul remembers
> And is bowed down within me.
> This I recall to my mind,
> Therefore I have hope.
> The Lord's lovingkindnesses indeed never cease,
> For His compassions never fail.
> They are new every morning;
> Great is Your faithfulness.
> 'The Lord is my portion,' says my soul,
> 'Therefore I have hope in Him.'"
>
> — Lamentations 3:19–24

As Jeremiah remembered who God is, hope was restored in his soul.

Second, we can call to mind specific promises or words we received from the Lord in the past. When the apostle Paul was on a ship in the middle of a bad storm, he kept his focus on a word that the Lord had given him. He even used that word to give hope to the men who traveled with him:

> "Yet now I urge you to keep up your courage, for there
> will be no loss of life among you, but only of the ship. For
> this very night an angel of the God to whom I belong and
> whom I serve stood before me, saying, 'Do not be afraid,
> Paul; you must stand before Caesar; and behold, God has
> granted you all those who are sailing with you.' Therefore,
> keep up your courage, men, for I believe God that it will
> turn out exactly as I have been told." — Acts 27:22–25

The third response to hopelessness is prayer—or what the Word of God describes as strengthening ourselves in the Lord. When David was experiencing hopelessness because his family had been kidnapped and his men wanted to stone him, he strengthened himself in the Lord:

"Moreover David was greatly distressed because the people spoke of stoning him, for all the people were embittered, each one because of his sons and his daughters. But David strengthened himself in the Lord his God."

— 1 Samuel 30:6

Once David had strengthened himself in the Lord, he was able to ask the Lord what he should do. Our God is always waiting to come to our side when we are in need.[9]

Finally, we can ask a brother or sister in the Lord to stand alongside us. That is the true meaning of comfort.[10]

Soulish Feelings of Condemnation Verses Conviction

"Beloved, if our heart does not condemn us, we have confidence before God." — 1 John 3:21

Two very common soulish emotions are the feeling of condemnation and the God-ordained feeling of conviction. We have to be able to tell the difference between these two diametrically opposed emotions. The devil is the author of condemnation,[11] whereas God uses the tool of conviction. He convicts the world of sin, but He convicts us, His children, of righteousness.[12] Feelings of condemnation are from the devil, but conviction is from God.

The Soulish Feeling of Condemnation

One time, I was ministering to a woman in her twenties whose father had abused her when she was young. The pain of those events tormented her heart. She had asked the Lord to heal her from that pain, but according to her, God was not answering her prayer.

I thought, That is not possible. I know my heavenly Father would come to her running. If my kids were hurting, I would come running.

Then it came to me: Her heart is condemning her! She did not have the confidence to approach God's Throne of Grace, so she was unable to receive the help she needed from Him.[13]

As we continued to talk, she revealed that she had bit into the lie that the abuse was her fault. She believed that if she had only done something, her dad would not have abused her. She believed she was the guilty and dirty one, when, clearly, it was not her fault—she could not have done anything about it. She was calling out to God with her conscious mind, but the programming of her heart was causing her spirit to turn away from Him, because she believed it was her fault. As she released the lie she believed to the Lord, I watched as God's love for her flooded her soul and His comfort filled her heart. She began to weep tears of relief.

Our loving heavenly Father does not force us to change our thoughts. Instead, He gently calls out to us, seeking to comfort us, while inviting us to release the lies that are condemning and wounding our hearts. This precious young woman had fallen into the devil's scheme of entertaining a condemning heart, which hindered her from going to the One who was able to heal her. The devil seeks to pour lies into our hearts so the emotions of condemnation will stop us from approaching the Throne of Grace, where an abundance of mercy and grace awaits us.

Condemnation is from three Greek words that communicate "to speak against" or "a judgment pronounced against." The feeling of condemnation, therefore, is our emotional state after we have been sorted out by a particular standard and found guilty. Since our God is absolutely holy, just, and righteous, it is very easy for the devil to accuse us of our shortcomings. In fact, Revelation 12:10 says he seeks to accuse us before God "day and night." When we accept the devil's sentence of guilt against us, he sets out to pile up the conclusions, and subsequently the feelings, of condemnation in our souls.

But Jesus, our Lord and Savior, intercedes on our behalf. *"Who is the one who condemns?"* Paul asks in Romans 8:34. *"Christ Jesus is He who died, yes, rather who was raised, who is at the right hand of God, who also intercedes for us."*

Our hearts and minds stand in the balance. They determine whether we will run to God for mercy and grace or withdraw from Him, entertaining thoughts and emotions of condemnation. That is one of the deadliest aspects of condemnation — it steals our confidence. Confidence is the soulish emotion that enables us to draw near to God; it is the reflection of our hearts' ability to speak and stand freely before Him:

> *"Therefore let us draw near with confidence to the throne of grace."*   — Hebrews 4:16

> *"Therefore, brethren, since we have confidence to enter the holy place by the blood of Jesus . . ."*
>   — Hebrews 10:19

When our hearts are confident in the finished work of Jesus Christ, we can boldly come to the Throne of Grace and receive what we need. The moment the enemy manages to con us out of confidently drawing near to God, he has won. Without confidence, we shrink away from God's holy presence[14] and can no longer access His resources to help us walk and live in victory.

We become subject to the feelings of condemnation for several reasons. One is the presence of unconfessed sin in our hearts, especially sins like rebellion[15] and pride.[11] However, both of these sins can be easily dealt with when we confess them to the Lord. Our God is rich in mercy,[16] ready to forgive us of our sins and release the freshness of His presence into our hearts.[17] He is there, waiting for us.

Condemnation can also affect our hearts when we inappropriately establish the Law of Moses as our foundation, rather than the love and faith of the Law of the Spirit of Life in Christ Jesus.[18] The Law of Moses is a law of outward obedience. It was and is a reminder of sin.[19] When we seek to be justified by our actions, the Law of Moses becomes a ministry of condemnation.[20]

The story I told at the beginning of this section reveals the most deadly type of condemnation: self-condemnation. A common form of self-condemnation occurs when we ask God to forgive us, but we do not agree with God's mercy and forgive ourselves. When we do not agree with God's mercy, we are agreeing with the devil's accusations. God calls us to come to Him and receive His mercy and grace, but when we are walking in self-condemnation, we do not allow ourselves to do so.

With every cause and form of condemnation, the important thing to remember is this: Condemnation is part of the devil's scheme to keep us from going to the One who is able, and willing, to give us mercy and grace.

The opposite of condemnation is justification and righteousness before God. When we accept Jesus' provision for our sins and stand by faith in the justification and righteousness found in Him, there is no condemnation for us: *"Therefore there is now no condemnation for those who are in Christ Jesus"* (Romans 8:1). We can come before the Throne of Grace with confidence.

The Soulish Feeling of Conviction

Conviction is completely different than condemnation. Conviction, or convict, is from the Greek word elégcho, which the NASB also translates as "reprove," "reproof," and "exposed." In John 3:20–21, Jesus used elégcho to describe people's works being "exposed by the light" (emphasis added):

> *"For everyone who does evil hates the Light, and does not come to the Light for fear that his deeds will be **exposed**. But he who practices the truth comes to the Light, so that his deeds may be manifested as having been wrought in God."*

When God convicts us of our mistakes, He allows the circumstances in our lives to bring our thoughts, words, and actions into the light. He does this as an act of love; Revelation 3:19 says He disciplines and reproves those He loves. God's conviction is not a cruel act of revengeful punishment—it is the heart of our heavenly Father wanting us to see what is trying to destroy us. When the things that would destroy us are brought into the light, we can lay them aside.

The Word of God tells us that when a sin or a problem is brought to the light and dealt with, the victory over that issue actually becomes light: *"But all things become visible when they are exposed by the light, for everything that becomes visible is light"* (Ephesians 5:13). Conviction is not condemnation by any means—it is our opportunity to allow the life of God to be released into our lives.

Conviction is part of our heavenly Father's disciplining process. His conviction empowers us and enables us to be "birthed" as His sons and daughters:

> *"My son, do not regard lightly the discipline of the Lord,*
> *Nor faint when you are reproved by Him*
> *For those whom the Lord loves He disciplines,*
> *And He scourges every son whom He receives."*
> — Hebrews 12:5-6

In other words, without God's conviction in our lives, we would be illegitimate children—we would be orphans and slaves, never living in His fullness as sons and daughters.

A few years ago, Ernie Tangalakis, one of my good friends, had a dream in which he and another man were taking a written test given by Ernie's dad. When they had finished, they turned the tests in to be graded. The other man aced the test, and Ernie's dad went to congratulate him. But then Ernie looked over at his dad's desk and saw his own test—he had failed. Immediately, he began to fear what his dad was going to say to him.

As his dad picked up the test and walked toward him, Ernie felt the fear of condemnation arise in his heart, but to his amazement, his dad didn't say a single negative word. Instead, he lovingly and patiently went over every mistake, bringing to light the things Ernie had done wrong and explaining how to do them right.

The dad in the dream represented God the Father, and as a result, the dream blessed my friend completely and gave him a new perspective on God's conviction. Again, His conviction does not condemn us for doing something wrong; His conviction brings the mistake to light so it can be changed. In other words, there is no reason for us to be afraid when God convicts us.

God's conviction is a vital part of our redemption process. Think about it like this: If something is not right, the best thing that could happen to us would be to discover what is wrong. We can then change what needs to be changed. We cannot change something when we ignorantly believe the wrong is a right.

The main way the Holy Spirit convicts us is by revealing to us what is righteous and true, not what is wrong with us:

> *"And He, when He comes, will convict the world concerning sin and righteousness and judgment; concerning sin, because they do not believe in Me; and concerning righteousness, because I go to the Father and you no longer see Me; and concerning judgment, because the ruler of this world has been judged."* — John 16:8–11

God convicts His children of righteousness. The revelation of God's righteousness and goodness leads us to repentance.[21]

When Isaiah saw the holiness of God, he realized he was a man of unclean lips — that is, he realized he was unholy:

> *"Then I said,*
> *'Woe is me, for I am ruined!*
> *Because I am a man of unclean lips,*
> *And I live among a people of unclean lips;*
> *For my eyes have seen the King, the Lord of hosts.'*
> *Then one of the seraphim flew to me with a burning coal in his hand, which he had taken from the altar with tongs.*

He touched my mouth with it and said, 'Behold, this has touched your lips; and your iniquity is taken away and your sin is forgiven.'
Then I heard the voice of the Lord, saying, 'Whom shall I send, and who will go for Us?' Then I said, 'Here am I. Send me!'" — Isaiah 6:5–8

No one had to tell Isaiah he was a man of unclean lips. The holiness of God made the man's unholiness very clear. His sin was brought to light not by the revelation that he was a sinner—but by the revelation of God's righteousness. Isaiah was cleansed of his sin, and he was commissioned in the area of redemption. He used to be a man of unclean lips, but after God's presence brought to light what needed to be brought to light, Isaiah was sent out to speak His truth. Our response to God's conviction is the key to overcoming the devil's schemes, and it also allows mercy and grace to be released into our lives.

Conviction and Confidence

"Therefore, do not throw away your confidence, which has a great reward." — Hebrews 10:35

We need to keep three factors in mind when we experience God's conviction. First, we need to guard the emotion of confidence in our hearts so we can continue to approach Him and seek His help.[13] He will never turn us away when we confidently come to Him in our time of need.

Second, we are to keep our eyes on God's truth.[22] When we take the eyes of our hearts off of Jesus, the devil has won because we will become what we look at. If we focus on our sins and trying to change our sins, our sins will become more and more entrenched in our hearts, but when we focus on the truth and glory of God, His truth and glory transform us into the "same image."

"But we all, with unveiled face, beholding as in a mirror the glory of the Lord, are being transformed into the same image from glory to glory, just as from the Lord, the Spirit."   — 2 Corinthians 3:18

"Beloved, now we are children of God, and it has not appeared as yet what we will be. We know that when He appears, we will be like Him, because we will see Him just as He is. And everyone who has this hope fixed on Him purifies himself, just as He is pure."   — 1 John 3:2–3

Finally, Hebrews 12:5 tells us we should not "faint." Literally, the word faint in this verse means to "loosen oneself from," which paints a picture in my mind of giving up. When my faults are brought into the light, it can be easy for me to feel like I am a hopeless case. If Jesus were not there to cover me, my heart wouldn't be able to take it. I need to hold on to my confidence in Jesus and what He did for me. When God's conviction reveals my sins and shortcomings, it is important that I confidently run into His presence, instead of running away. There I can find mercy for my mistakes and grace to overcome the things that are trying to hold me back.

Every time we sense condemnation, it is from the devil. In response, we need to raise the shield of faith so we will be able to extinguish all the fiery darts of darkness and run to our God. God's conviction is not there to condemn us — but to heal us and set us free. It is full of life.

Soulish Feelings of Intimacy Versus Shame

"And the man and his wife were both naked and were not ashamed."   — Genesis 2:25

God created us to walk in intimacy with Him and others. Before Adam and Eve sinned, they knew that level of intimacy, and because they walked closely with God, there was no shame in their lives. I heard a brother say that intimacy means "into me see." Adam and Eve were completely vulnerable with God and each other. They lived in such a way that they were unafraid for God to see everything about them. There was nothing hidden in their lives, and they lived in the light of God's love and holiness.

> *"If we walk in the Light as He Himself is in the Light, we have fellowship with one another, and the blood of Jesus His Son cleanses us from all sin."* — 1 John 1:7

When we live in intimacy with God and others, we are living in His presence. His fullness can easily flow into our lives and relationships. God's love casts out all of our fears, and our relationships are permeated with belief and trust. As a result of the love and faith brought by intimacy, joy and peace become part of the fabric of our lives.

The Soulish Emotion of Shame

The antithesis of intimacy is shame. Shame is a devastating emotion that can destroy us, as well as our relationships. Paul describes shame as something that "hides":

> *"We have renounced the things hidden because of shame, not walking in craftiness or adulterating the word of God, but by the manifestation of truth commending ourselves to every man's conscience in the sight of God."* — 2 Corinthians 4:2

John affirms this description of shame in 1 John 2:28: *"Now, little children, abide in Him, so that when He appears, we may have confidence and not shrink away from Him in shame at His coming."* When Adam and Eve sinned in the Garden of Eden, they shrunk back and hid themselves from God, but He sought them out, asking, "Where are you?" He wanted them to reveal themselves to Him.[23] Shame carries with it the fear of being exposed; we want to hide ourselves and the sin or issue causing us to feel this way. I have watched many brothers and sisters allow shame to push them into isolation and withdrawal from God and others; this keeps them from completing the call of God on their lives.

Religious structures and the world both use shame as a motivation not to sin. But in reality, shame empowers our sins. As a child when I did something I should not have done, I remember hearing people say, "Shame on you!" Those verbal curses of shame were very powerful weapons in my life.

We can feel shame when we do not measure up to a particular standard of living, and we can also feel shame when someone we love does not measure up to that standard. I have heard numerous testimonies of people who struggled with poverty or addictions. Shame haunted their hearts and the hearts of their family members as well.

Jesus Christ is holy. Because of our sins and ungodliness, He has every right to be ashamed of us, but the good news is that our Savior is not ashamed to call us His brothers and sisters.[24] With the power of His redeeming love, He causes us to overcome the temptation of entertaining shame. Like He did with the woman caught in adultery, He stands with us before our accusers and picks us up.[25] Then He empowers us to overcome our disappointments, including the disappointment we feel toward ourselves.

When our confidence is placed in God's love and redemption, we come into the light so He can redeem and establish us in His love. In the hands of God, there is no shame; there is only complete and unhindered intimacy with Him and others. His heart breaks both for the addict and the family of the addict, and He wants to redeem, heal, empower, and comfort. Our God so loves us that the sheer force of His redeeming love can bring us out of hiding and allow us to experience true intimacy.

Soulish Feelings of Godly Sorrow Versus Worldly Sorrow

Another important soulish emotion is that of sorrow. There are two types of sorrow. Godly sorrow is in line with the Spirit and has hope. The second type of sorrow is that of the world, and it produces hopelessness, condemnation, and death.

Paul mentions these two opposing types of sorrow in 2 Corinthians 7:9–11:

> *"I now rejoice, not that you were made sorrowful, but that you were made sorrowful to the point of repentance; for you were made sorrowful according to the will of God, so that you might not suffer loss in anything through us. For the sorrow that is according to the will of God produces a repentance without regret, leading to salvation, but the sorrow of the world produces death. For behold what earnestness this very thing, this godly sorrow, has produced in you: what vindication of yourselves, what indignation, what fear, what longing, what zeal, what avenging of wrong! In everything you demonstrated yourselves to be innocent in the matter."*

Let's look at both of these types of sorrow a little more closely.

Soulish Feelings of Godly Sorrow

Godly sorrow *"produces a repentance without regret, leading to salvation."* Godly sorrow is the emotion that occurs when we realize we have sinned. It empowers us to turn quickly to our Savior for redemption and reconciliation so we "might not suffer loss in anything."

The Greek word for repentance literally means "another mind." The sorrow of God causes us to think differently about sin, His mercy, and His grace. With godly sorrow, there is no guilt or condemnation; instead, we are concerned about how to make things right before Him and other people. There is no regret either, because we know God's mercy and grace overcome our mistakes.[26] This type of sorrow produces a mindset that looks forward to God's redemption and salvation and does not look back in remorse. It also does not have an attitude of vindication, anger, fear, or defending oneself.

When I think of godly sorrow, I think of King David. Every time David was convicted of his sin, sorrow resulted, but in his sorrow, he always looked forward to God's redemption and what God was about to do as a result of His redemption. For instance, when David sinned with Bathsheba and their baby died, he looked forward to God's redemption in Heaven.[27] Later when David sinned by taking a census of his people, he sought God's mercy with his whole heart and offered a sacrifice to Him on the threshing floor of Ornan. Then after receiving God's mercy, he pressed forward toward God's redemption and restoration, this time by making preparations to build the temple.[28] Every time David sinned, he ran to God. Because of God's redeeming power, every sin became an opportunity for God's grace and mercy to be manifested in his life. Godly sorrow always produces repentance that leads to life.

Soulish Feelings of Worldly Sorrow

The sorrow of the world is the opposite of godly sorrow. Worldly sorrow produces death, which is a picture of separation — the sorrow of the world pushes us to separate ourselves from God and people. Guilt and condemnation are common with this type of sorrow, and often there is a strong urge to defend ourselves.

The basis of worldly sorrow is loss. We look back in regret. There is no faith in God's redemption — there is just a focus on the fact that we were caught in sin. My personal belief is that this type of emotion can easily lead to various forms of fear and depression. Our souls fill with the fear of loss, either a loss that has already occurred or a loss that could occur.

In religious circles, it is easy to confuse godly sorrow and worldly sorrow. All of us make mistakes, and in the aftermath, the sorrow we entertain can make us or break us. It is important for us to understand the two types of soulish sorrow and their unique differences. If we embrace godly sorrow, our Father's redemption and reconciliation will take over, and that sorrow will eventually be turned to joy.

Soulish Feelings and Physical Pain

When our physical bodies are in pain, our minds and hearts become vulnerable to the attacks of the enemy, and it is easy for him to shoot fiery darts into our thoughts. When the physical pain is intense, thoughts about what we have done wrong, our sins, or our lack of faith can begin to permeate our hearts and minds. The enemy will also try to attack our beliefs about the nature and character of God. Our thoughts can cause bitterness to fill our souls.

When the devil was physically tormenting him, the soulish emotion of bitterness weighed heavily upon Job:

> *"I loathe my own life;*
> *I will give full vent to my complaint;*
> *I will speak in the bitterness of my soul.*
> *I will say to God, 'Do not condemn me;*
> *Let me know why You contend with me.*
> *'Is it right for You indeed to oppress,*
> *To reject the labor of Your hands,*
> *And to look favorably on the schemes of the wicked?'"*
> — Job 10:1-3

In the context of his physical pain, there was no rest for Job's soul because he believed the Lord was oppressing him while blessing evildoers. The Lord had not abandoned Job, nor was it the Lord who was oppressing him. In truth, the Lord was compassionate and merciful to him: *"We count those blessed who endured. You have heard of the endurance of Job and have seen the outcome of the Lord's dealings, that the Lord is full of compassion and is merciful"* (James 5:11).

Job's soul could have found rest if he had been able to grasp the truth that God was his safe place, not the inflictor of his pain. Several times when I was very sick, my soul had no rest because I was entertaining a lie that something was innately wrong with me or that God was mad at me. In those times, my soul was tormented and troubled. But at other times, I have known my heavenly Father is with me and that He is my healer. Even though my body was hurting and my mind was delirious from the fever or pain, there was peace, joy, and love in my soul.

One of my convictions is that when we have been injured or are intensely sick, we should not spend time trying to decide whether or not we are in sin or what we did wrong to end up that way. If we have sinned, the Lord can reveal it to us out of a place of rest and not torture—He does not condemn us concerning our sins. When we are in pain, the focus of our minds and hearts needs to be on the nature and character of our loving and faithful God.

Soulish Feelings of Being Forsaken

When Jesus walked the earth, He was tempted in everything we are tempted in. On the cross, He felt something that most of us have felt at one time or another: the feeling of being forsaken or abandoned.

He cried out, "Eli, Eli, lama sabachthani?" which means, "My God, My God, why have You forsaken Me?" Having taken on our sufferings, sicknesses, physical pain, mental pain, depressions, sins, and rebellions, He felt like the Father had left Him.[29] But the Father never left Him. Just before Jesus was to be betrayed, tried, beaten, and taken to the cross, He proclaimed,

> *"Behold, an hour is coming, and has already come, for*
> *you to be scattered, each to his own home, and to leave Me*
> *alone; and yet I am not alone, because the Father is with*
> *Me."*   — John 16:32

I know it is traditionally taught (I have even taught it) that God the Father had to turn away from Jesus on the cross because Jesus had taken on our sins. Because of John 16:32, I now believe that teaching is not true. Before the tribulations of the cross hit Jesus in full force, He knew the Father would not leave Him, but our pain and sin clouded His ability to see the Father.

Notice the effects of sin recorded in Isaiah 59:1–2:

> *"Behold, the Lord's hand is not so short*
> *That it cannot save;*
> *Nor is His ear so dull*
> *That it cannot hear.*
> *But your iniquities have made*
> *a separation between you and your God,*
> *And your sins have hidden His face from you so that He*
> *does not hear."*

Our sins hide God's face from us. They hinder our ability to hear the Lord speaking. I know the English version of Scripture concludes the last sentence of this passage with *"so that He does not hear."* However, when you take the whole passage and put it together, God is always able to save and hear, but our sins and iniquities hinder our ability to see and hear Him. So when Jesus took our sins and pain on the cross, He felt what we feel when sin and pain attack our souls—He felt like God the Father had left Him.

God promises us, "I will never desert you, nor will I ever forsake you." When we sin, the Lord pursues us. He will leave the ninety-nine and go after the one who has gone astray.[30] Many of us have experienced the loneliness of depression; we have felt the despair and condemnation of unconfessed sin, but our heavenly Father will never leave us. He will pursue us in those dark times.

As a father in both the natural and spiritual realms, when a son or daughter of mine messes up, my heart is not to abandon that person; my heart is for pursuit. Jesus tells us that when one sheep goes astray, He will leave the ninety-nine to pursue the one who is lost. God's heart is not to abandon us in our sins or dark moments—but for redemption to come into our lives. Like the father in the parable of the prodigal son, even if He has to let us go, He does so that we may gain revelation concerning the fruitlessness of our sin and the effects of sin and death.

Ultimately, the question is not whether or not God sees or pursues us—it is if we can see and hear Him. Our soulish emotions start interpreting our environment, and it is easy to feel things that are not based in truth. Because of those emotions, we can be pushed to take actions that we will later regret—actions that are unnecessary because God is always with us.

Soulish Feelings of Trauma

When the Amalekites kidnapped the families of David and his men, he and his men grieved until they had no strength left in them.[31] For a time, those emotions of grief were not processed correctly, and the men allowed themselves to become bitter. They started talking about stoning David:

> "Moreover David was greatly distressed because the people spoke of stoning him, for all the people were embittered [literally "bitter of soul"], each one because of his sons and his daughters. But David strengthened himself in the Lord his God." — 1 Samuel 30:6

David, who was hurting just as much as his men, did not allow his grief to become bitterness. It would have been easy for him just to give up. Or he could have turned to anger and sought to divide his men by fighting with them. Instead, he went to the Lord and strengthened himself in Him, so he could accurately hear and see what God was doing. When the emotions of trauma fill our souls, it is important for us to turn to the Lord and allow His presence to comfort and strengthen us. Our God is a God of comfort and peace.

Years later when Jeremiah was watching the enemy ransack his beloved country, he experienced a number of disturbing emotions.[32] We looked at his hopelessness earlier in this chapter. In the beginning, the trauma tormented his soul, but as time progressed, Jeremiah turned his mind and heart to focus on the Lord's nature and character, and hope started to fill him.

Jeremiah knew that God is a good God. He knew God is a God of lovingkindness, faithfulness, and compassion. We need to allow the reality of these truths to permeate our souls. In times and seasons of trauma, the truth of God's nature and character provides an anchor for us. That anchor brings great stability to shattered and battered hearts and minds.

Again, when we experience a traumatic event, it is important for us not to allow the emotions generated by that event to push our minds and hearts into ungodly thoughts and actions. Instead, we need to rest in the Lord and who He is. That is how we battle these times.

Soulish Feelings of Fear

All of us know what fear feels like. Some of us have experienced it so intensely that we've shut down emotionally, perhaps even physically. Fear is one of the most powerful emotions we will ever deal with. Fear has both physical and spiritual emotions, but in this section, we will focus primarily on the soulish emotion of fear.

This is my working definition of the soulish emotion of fear:

Fear is an emotion that signals a belief, conclusion, or realization that we, or someone we care about, are in an environment of danger, intimidation, vulnerability, helplessness, or being overwhelmed.

Scripture supports this definition in both the Old and New Testaments. Moses felt fear because he believed he was vulnerable in God's presence and could be destroyed:

> *"I fell down before the Lord, as at the first, forty days and nights; I neither ate bread nor drank water, because of all your sin which you had committed in doing what was evil in the sight of the LORD to provoke Him to anger. For* **I was afraid of the anger and hot displeasure with which the LORD was wrathful against you in order to destroy you,** *but the LORD listened to me that time also."* — Deuteronomy 9:18–19, (emphasis added)

The children of Israel felt fear because they believed they were helpless before the giants in the Promised Land:

> *"Only do not rebel against the LORD; and* **do not fear the people of the land, for they will be our prey.** *Their protection has been removed from them, and the Lord is with us; do not fear them."*
> — Numbers 14:9, (emphasis added)

Two things need to be taken into account when we consider the emotion of fear: the internal (our hearts) and the external (our environment). We need to ask ourselves, "What is going on around me?" And, "What is going on in me as I evaluate what is going on around me?"

Fear is an emotion like any other, and as we know, an emotion is a signal of an event. In the case of soulish fear, the event occurs as a person encounters an environment that makes them feel helpless, vulnerable, or intimidated.

Dangerous Environments

Fear is a "natural" result of living in a fallen world. When Adam and Eve sinned, their actions set loose a worldwide condition of sin and death, which separated creation from God's love and security. Fear, therefore, became a reality in every created being, physical and spiritual. Every part of this world experiences at least some of the effects of sin and death. Danger and vulnerability permeate this realm. Ever since the first sin, the human race has lived with the reality of some type of fear, including the fear of approaching God:

> *"Then the Lord God called to the man, and said to him, 'Where are you?' He said, 'I heard the sound of You in the garden, and I was afraid because I was naked; so I hid myself.'"* — Genesis 3:9–10

When sin and death were fully realized after Noah's flood, animals started living with the reality of fear:

> *"The fear of you and the terror of you will be on every beast of the earth and on every bird of the sky; with everything that creeps on the ground, and all the fish of the sea, into your hand they are given."* — Genesis 9:2

Fear even started effecting spiritual beings, including demons. They live in fear of God's justice and righteousness because they have embraced sin and death:

> *"And they cried out, saying, 'What business do we have with each other, Son of God? Have You come here to torment us before the time?'"* — Matthew 8:29

> *"You believe that God is one. You do well; the demons also believe, and shudder."* — James 2:19

All of creation is threatened with danger and intimidation and therefore suffers fear, but according to Galatians 1:4,

Jesus came to deliver us out of this present evil age. He came to deliver us from fear so we can live in the fullness of a loving God.[33]

We have the opportunity to live dependent on God and victorious over the enslavement of fear; however, we have not wholly realized the fullness of the deliverance Jesus provided. So every day we live in some form of danger or intimidation, dealing with a variety of threats. We worry. We fear. What if we are in a car accident? What if we get sick? What if we lose something or someone we value? Fear permeates the world — but thanks to God, we have the opportunity to overcome fear through His presence and provision.

Our Response to the Environment

How do your mind and heart evaluate your environment?

We become afraid when we encounter an event that makes us believe that we, or someone we care about, is in an environment of danger, helplessness, vulnerability, or intimidation. As a result of the environment, a conclusion in our hearts is brought to light by the emotion of fear. Often, that conclusion is doubt.

In Matthew 14, Peter started with faith. Jesus invited him to get out of the boat and join Him on the surface of the lake. And Peter did. He walked on the water as if it were a solid road, but because of the storm raging around him, doubt began to divide the focus of his heart:

> *"But seeing the wind, [Peter] became frightened, and beginning to sink, he cried out, 'Lord, save me!'. . . Immediately Jesus stretched out His hand and took hold of him, and said to him, 'You of little faith, why did you doubt?'"* — Matthew 14:30–31

Doubt means divided judgments. When we doubt, we are focusing on the apparent "facts" and not on God's truth.

When Peter saw the wind, fear started filling his soul, and he began to sink. He started to believe that he was in danger, helpless, and vulnerable. His doubt threw open the door to fear. Doubt was the first thing to affect Peter; then as the emotion of fear arose, it stole his ability to rest in the power of Jesus' word. Whenever I sense fear in myself, I try to stop and remember that it means my heart is in a state of doubt.

All of us, if we wanted to, could find many reasons to be afraid in this life. Satan is the ruler of this world.[34] If the world sought to intimidate and destroy Jesus, and keep Him from His mission to bring the Father's children out of darkness, it will certainly seek to intimidate and destroy us.[35] When we start declaring God's goodness and delivering people out of the devil's authority, we can expect the devil to try to intimidate us and keep us from that mission.

But Jesus encourages us not to allow the world to make us feel vulnerable or helpless. Our Father will judge on our behalf. The greatness and awesomeness of our God will become evident. He will bring everything into the light and fight for us, so we can overcome the fears generated by the adversities of this world.

We cannot escape the world's adversities and dangerous environments, but we can keep our faith filled with revelations of God and the truth of His Word. That is what David did in Psalm 32:6–7:

> *"Therefore, let everyone who is godly pray to You in a*
> *time when You may be found;*
> *Surely in a flood of great waters they will not reach him.*
> *You are my hiding place; You preserve me from trouble;*
> *You surround me with songs of deliverance."*

David knew that God is far bigger than any adversity we could ever face. God is greater than any environment in this world. If our God is for us, who can be against us?[36] What can separate us from His love?[37]

There is no adversity or environment on earth that can separate us from our Father's love; therefore, our fears can be cast out.[38] Also, there is no adversity or environment on earth that can separate us from our Father's care or keep Him from giving us victory. So we have no reason to be afraid.

Good Fear Versus Bad Fear

I used to boast that I would love to see Jesus face to face. But I don't do that anymore! One night several years ago, I was lying in bed worshiping the Lord. Paula had gone to visit her parents, and I was alone. My eyes were closed.

Out of the blue, I heard a voice speak to me: "Open your eyes, and you can see Jesus."

Immediately, I started thinking, You mean, the Lord of Lords. The Prince of Peace. The Mighty God . . . The revelation of His greatness filled me, and fear and reverence started overcoming my mind and heart. In the end, I grabbed the blankets, pulled them up over my head, and yelled, "No!" I was scared. To this day, I don't know whether Jesus was standing there in my room or not, but I do know that the revelation of His awesomeness overwhelmed me, and as a result, the emotion of fear filled my soul.

Throughout God's Word, we find examples of people who experienced a form of fear whenever God's awe-inspiring nature and character were revealed to them. When the fear of God came upon them, it usually produced a positive, inspiring response in their lives.[39] Remember that the basic foundations of fear are thoughts of helplessness, vulnerability, and being overwhelmed. Interestingly, those types of thoughts are also the foundation for humility. When we are helpless or vulnerable before God, it is a revelation that He is the greater One; He is more than we are, and that understanding produces humility. With God, humility is the doorway through which we receive grace and exaltation, so a healthy fear of the Lord has a positive effect on our faith. It instills within us a heart to worship Him and give Him honor. In the Book of Proverbs, Solomon reiterated that important concept: *"By lovingkindness and truth iniquity is atoned for, and by the fear of the Lord one keeps away from evil"* (Proverbs 16:6).

Being fearful is not always a negative experience. There is good fear, and there is bad fear. The key difference between them is the fruit they generate in our lives. Our response to good fear can lead us to life, while our response to bad fear can lead us into forms of death.

Several times in Scripture when Jesus revealed Himself, or when an angel of the Lord appeared to someone, He said right away, "Do not be afraid." This happened repeatedly in Matthew and Luke; we can also find it in Mark, John, and Revelation. The revelation of God's greatness produces reverence and awe that will lead people, things, and spiritual beings to forms of praise and worship.[40] God created the heavens and the earth.[41] He holds everything together.[42] Everything that sees Him is humbled at the sight and sound of Him. He veils Himself to us so that our acceptance of Him comes from hearts of love and the freedom of choice; however, the moment our senses begin to register His greatness in some way, we cannot help but feel a measure of fear. Our first glance of His greatness can easily cause us to feel vulnerable, helpless, and overwhelmed.

When Jesus raised a young man from the dead, the people who witnessed it became afraid:

> *"The dead man sat up and began to speak. And Jesus gave him back to his mother. **Fear gripped them all, and they began glorifying God, saying**, 'A great prophet has arisen among us!' and, 'God has visited His people!'"*
> — Luke 7:15–16, (emphasis added)

Fear arose in their hearts, and they responded by glorifying God; they declared truths about Jesus and the reality that God was with them, and these responses brought life into their situation.

When God's power and awesomeness are manifested, it is an event that humbles us and makes us feel weak in light of His greatness. God is truly awesome, and He wants us to know Him in light of His awesomeness — but that is not all He wants us to know. If His greatness were the only revelation of God we had, our relationship with Him would be based solely on fear, reverence, and awe. And that is not what He wants. He is drawing us deeper into His heart, where our relationship with Him treasures the power of who He is but also grasps His tenderness, lovingkindness, and compassion. That balancing act demands a supernatural relationship.

The main difference between the "good fear" of God and the "bad fear" of God is in our foundational beliefs of Him and the responses generated by our fear. The fear of God is a good fear when our conclusions about Him are revelations of truth about the greatness of who He is; these conclusions generate responses of faith, love, reverence, and worship within us. Proverbs 14:26 says, *"In the fear of the Lord there is strong confidence."*

What I call the bad fear of God occurs when the conclusions about Him in our hearts are based on untruths; these conclusions cause us to respond in unbelief and unholiness. For example, if people are taught that God is only a God of wrath and judgment, the residual effects of that fear lead them into bondage.

On the other end of the spectrum, when we realize that God's wrath and judgment are expressions of His love for us and His compassion against pain, sorrow, and injustice — that kind of "fear" leads to respect and honor. Jesus became angry with the religious leaders of His day because they had a greater desire to protect their religious order than see a person healed and comforted.[43] Jesus' anger was the result of the injustice of religion. Whenever we hear about God's wrath, we need to understand that wrath is His loving heart being broken for the sin, death, and injustices that have occurred or are occurring in the world.

In order to walk in the fear of the Lord that leads to life, we have to have conclusions about Him in our hearts that are consistent with the fullness of His character: love, grace, mercy, life — as well as judgment, wrath, and justice. We cannot healthily consider His judgment, wrath, and justice without also integrating His love, grace, mercy, and life.

So good fear draws us closer to God, while bad fear creates obstacles of doubt and unbelief in our hearts and minds. As our faith begins to wilt, we experience a form of spiritual death brought on by fear. Good fear always brings life, while bad fear always produces some sort of death.

How to Deal with Fear

I have heard numerous testimonies of soldiers who, in the midst of very intense battles, had to fend off the enslaving effects of fear in order to respond courageously to the situation. It was not that they stopped feeling the emotions of fear that were signaling the danger; it was that they didn't allow the signals of their hearts to lead them into defeat.

Remember our two main questions when we are dealing with emotions: What is being signaled? And how do we respond? When we are in dangerous situations, our souls are correctly discerning and interpreting what is going on around us — but we do not have to allow that signal to push us into unbelief or defeat.

In a lot of cases, if we sense fear in our hearts, it means we have encountered an environment that is revealing a specific area within us that hasn't yet been redeemed. Our hearts "program" our spirits and essentially tell them how to function. According to Romans 8:15, a heart with the programming of a slave (that is, the person thinks like a slave) will have difficulty understanding God as his or her Father and will deal with fear. But Jesus wants us to be able to embrace our adoption as God's sons and daughters. As children of God, we can come into our Father's presence in love, not in fear:

> *"For you have not received a spirit of slavery leading to fear again, but you have received a spirit of adoption as sons by which we cry out, 'Abba! Father!'"*
> — Romans 8:15

The perfected love of the Father will cast out our fear. We will be able to draw near to Him as confident sons and daughters, looking for His abundant grace and mercy.

Whenever our hearts begin to sense fear, it is important to take note of what we are thinking in the midst of that fear. If the fear is generating within us an awe or reverence for God, we need to open ourselves to what God is showing us and express praise, thanksgiving, or worship. But if the fear is causing us to doubt God's character, we need to respond immediately and take our thoughts captive, so we can focus on the truth.

God's heart is that we would use fear as a signal that something is amiss in our hearts. When we feel afraid, why are we afraid? What false conclusion about God are we dealing with? If we can rightly discern what the fear is signaling, we can allow the Lord to minister into our hearts the truth of who He is and what He does. As this happens, we will experience a love that is beyond imagination.

Key Points of Chapter 5

I daresay every one of us has experienced most, if not all, of the emotions discussed in this chapter. I wanted to go over these common emotions here near the beginning of the book so you can start to identify what you are experiencing or have experienced in the past. Once you identify the emotional signals, you can then start to understand how to process those emotions.

What does a lie feel like? What does truth feel like? God created the human heart with the capacity to tell when a deadly lie has penetrated it. When we discern the lie, we can appropriately respond and remove it from our hearts.

No Condemnation

Every time we sense condemnation, it is from the devil. In response, we need to raise the shield of faith so we will be able to extinguish all the fiery darts of darkness and run to God.

We Are Not Deserted

God promises us, "I will never desert you, nor will I ever forsake you." When we sin, the Lord pursues us. He will leave the ninety-nine and go after the one who has gone astray. Our heavenly Father will never leave us. He will seek us out even in dark times.

We Can Stabilize Ourselves in God

When the emotions of trauma fill our souls, it is important for us to turn to the Lord and allow His presence to comfort and strengthen us. The truth of God's nature and character is an anchor that brings great stability to broken hearts and minds.

Notes / Reference Scriptures

1. Hebrews 5:14
2. Romans 8:28
3. 2 Corinthians 2:14
4. 1 Peter 5:7
5. Philippians 4:6-7
6. Isaiah 26:3
7. Hebrews 6:19
8. Hebrews 13:5
9. Isaiah 30:18
10. Matthew 26:38
11. 1 Timothy 3:6
12. John 16:8-11
13. Hebrews 4:16
14. 1 John 2:28
15. Romans 13:2
16. Ephesians 2:4
17. Acts 3:19
18. Romans 8:2
19. Hebrews 10:1-3
20. 2 Corinthians 3:7-9
21. Romans 2:4
22. Hebrews 12:2
23. Genesis 3:7-10
24. Hebrews 2:11
25. John 8:1-11
26. Romans 5:20
27. 2 Samuel 12:23
28. 1 Chronicles 22
29. Matthew 27:46
30. Luke 15:2-4
31. 1 Samuel 30:4
32. Lamentations 3:17-24
33. Hebrews 2:12-15
34. John 12:31
35. John 15:18
36. Romans 8:31
37. Romans 8:35-39
38. 1 John 4:18
39. Luke 5:25-26
40. Isaiah 55:11-12
41. Colossians 1:16
42. Colossians 1:17
43. Mark 3:2-5

What Does the Soulish Emotions Mean?

6

A good friend of mine was abused as a child. As a result of that abuse, she struggled with overwhelming emotions and would take actions that were detrimental to her and her close family relationships. Some suggested that maybe she needed medication to help level out what she was feeling.

One day when the emotions had reached a peak, we ministered to her, and the Lord gently and lovingly revealed that the emotions she had been dealing with signaled false conclusions in her heart concerning weakness and comfort. For her, weakness meant vulnerability and susceptibility to pain and abuse. She had never experienced true biblical comfort, where God was her strength. Because of the abuse in her past, the concepts of weakness and comfort were very negative concepts in her thinking. Her conclusions were causing her to experience all kinds of negative emotions, which hindered her from embracing the power of biblical weakness:

> "He has said to me, 'My grace is sufficient for you, for power is perfected in weakness.' Most gladly, therefore, I will rather boast about my weaknesses, so that the power of Christ may dwell in me. Therefore I am well content with weaknesses, with insults, with distresses, with per-

secutions, with difficulties, for Christ's sake; for when I
am weak, then I am strong."

— 2 Corinthians 12:9–10

The Lord powerfully healed her heart of those conclusions, and she was able to embrace the truth of God concerning biblical weakness. She received God's comfort and peace, which brought stability to her soul.

When we have judged that the emotion we feel is a soulish emotion, we next need to discern:

1. If the emotion is coming from a belief in our hearts,
2. If it is a stored emotion, or
3. If it reveals where our souls are anchored.

Most of the time, we feel soulish emotions because our conscious minds are using our beliefs to interpret a current environment or event or an environment/event we experienced in the past.

Is the Emotion Signaling a Belief?

In Psalm 63, David experienced positive soulish emotions even though he was hiding for his life from King Saul in a wilderness:

"My soul is satisfied as with marrow and fatness,
And my mouth offers praises with joyful lips.
When I remember You on my bed,
I meditate on You in the night watches,
*For **You have been my help**,*
And in the shadow of Your wings I sing for joy.
My soul clings to You;
Your right hand upholds me.
But those who seek my life to destroy it,
Will go into the depths of the earth."

— Psalm 63:2–9, (emphasis added)

Notice that in the midst of adversity, David called the past to mind. He said he would *"meditate on You . . . for You have been my help."* As a result, he experienced positive emotions like satisfaction and joy. These soulish emotions came from a conclusion—a belief in his heart. He knew the Lord was his help; therefore, even in a wilderness, David was able to sing for joy.

One Friday night, I received a call from a student in our campus ministry. She told me she was struggling with intense feelings of loneliness. I asked what she was doing, and she said she was sitting in her dorm room watching her friends go out on dates. During our conversation, she realized her feelings of loneliness were coming from the conclusions she had in her heart about being alone. The truth of the matter was that she was not alone—Jesus was with her. As she dealt with the belief in her heart, the loneliness started to subside.

In that example, my friend's thoughts were focused on the fact that she was not "with" anyone; because of her focus, she was dealing with loneliness. In that moment, this was the question she needed to answer: "What is hindering your heart from focusing on the truth that Jesus is with you?" She was not alone, but the truth of Jesus' presence could not release joy into her heart. Her beliefs about loneliness had been fashioned by past abandonments and betrayals, and her doubts were making it difficult for her to "feel" God's presence. As I ministered to her on the phone, she found freedom from past hurts and was able to focus her mind on God's truth. It is possible for us to feel lonely in a room filled with people because of our beliefs.

Sometimes the beliefs generating an emotion are so deep that the conscious mind has no recollection of the event that caused those beliefs. This often happens with people who were abused. They can experience a variety of strong emotions and have no idea where the feelings are coming from. The event occurred so long ago or was so traumatic that their conscious minds do not remember it. In that case, it is very important to use the tools God has given us to unearth these events and the beliefs that came out of them.^A

The best way we can determine if the soulish emotion is coming from a belief or from a momentary focus of the mind is to evaluate the thoughts we were thinking before and during the emotion. If our thoughts had nothing to do with the emotion, it most likely is not a soulish emotion. However, if the emotion correlates to our thoughts, it likely is a soulish emotion, and just as likely, it is based on the beliefs of our hearts.

When we are able to make that diagnosis and address the beliefs that hinder us, we are no longer subject to the devil's schemes, tossed around emotionally and swamped with feelings of instability.

Is the Emotion Signaling a Stored Emotion?

Our souls can produce stored emotions. When an emotional event occurs, the heart stores the conclusion of the event (what we believe about it), as well as the emotions experienced during the event.

I knew a woman in her fifties who would go into a fearful panic every time she saw the new pastor of her church. As we ministered to her, we discovered that her dad had sexually abused her when she was a little girl, and the new pastor happened to look just like her dad. So when she saw her pastor, all of the emotions and memories of the abuse flooded her soul. We were able to participate with the Lord as He healed her heart. He freed her to interact with her pastor. Our emotions are capable of engraving "facts" on our hearts. I have to be careful when I listen to music from the '60s and '70s because of all the emotional memories they stir up within me, both positive and negative. I can remember what I was feeling when I used to listen to those songs, and if I over-focus on them, it can lead me into pits of nostalgia.

In Psalm 63, the stored emotions were positive. David had seen God's power and glory in the past; he had felt the lovingkindness and joy of God's presence. Later in the wilderness, he could recall those events and their emotions and use them to refresh his faith and hope in God.

It is very important for us to deal with the conclusions of our hearts and the events that generated those conclusions. A significant part of freeing ourselves from the pain of the past is dealing with issues of forgiveness.

Emotions and Forgiveness

If I have a splinter in my hand, I can find it without too much effort. It will make its presence known when I rub my skin. If the Holy Spirit is tenderly "rubbing" our hearts and we lose our peace or feel pain in regard to an event, we have a "splinter" — there is something that needs to be healed.

When a person hurts us or someone we love, the devil will often try to entice us to hold that painful memory in our hearts. The act of holding to that painful memory is called unforgiveness. In my experience, unforgiveness is the number one sin used by the powers of darkness to gain a legal right to harass people.

God is so sure and steadfast that we can put absolute confidence in Him and His processes. Because God and His Word are so faithful, we can expect to have peace, love, and joy in our hearts after we have prayed through forgiveness issues. If we do not have peace, love, and joy after such prayers, there is something else we need to pray about.

When dealing with our emotions and issues of forgiveness, we need to keep these two points in mind:

1. Very often, people think all they have to do is forgive the person for wronging them. But when someone has sinned against us, we also need to ask God to forgive us for any unrighteous responses we had in the midst of our pain. These responses could be anger, bitterness, complaining, hatred, judgment, rebellion, etc.

2. The same event can produce multiple areas of hurt and lies in our lives. One event can come at us from many different angles. For example, when a dad divorces a mom and abandons his kids, the divorce is a single event, but the kids likely will have to deal with several different lies. If the children forgive the dad only for the divorce, they could still walk through life with a great deal of pain. Peace is the key. If there is no peace after praying through forgiveness, it likely is a signal that there is more to the event.

When we hold on to the offenses and wrongs of others, it opens a door for further pain and suffering to enter our lives. Many times in counseling sessions, I think to myself how unfair it is that this person is so tormented by a sin committed against him or her. The one who injured this person so severely seems to live guilt-free, while the one wronged is haunted by the past. But as I think about this, I remember the truth that Satan is the ruler of this world,[1] and his desire is to kill and enslave people with sinful acts. Unforgiveness is one of Satan's schemes.[2] As long as we are holding on to unforgiveness, it gives the powers of darkness legal right to torment us.[3] When we do not forgive an offense, we become enslaved to that event. Wherever we go, we drag the emotions of that offense with us. We see current and future events through those emotions and a filter of unforgiveness.

We forgive the ones who have wronged us in order to free ourselves from the painful emotions of past hurts. This will enable us to more accurately deal with future hurts as well.

The measure of forgiveness we extend to others is the measure of forgiveness we receive.[4] But here's the interesting thing: Unforgiveness is not for the person who committed the offense—but for the one who suffered the offense. It is not for the offender but for the one who was offended. When we forgive someone who has wronged us, we are not saying that his or her actions were acceptable or didn't really matter. We are saying that we want our hearts to be free from the offense's pain and frustration. The Lord's command to forgive is the expression of His heart. He wants us to be free from the painful events of the past. We do not have to carry these emotions with us—we can choose to forgive.

Don't Wait for the Feelings to Come—Choose to Forgive

Often, people want to feel like forgiving before they forgive, but forgiveness is not a feeling—it is a choice to obey God. The Greek word for forgive is in imperative tense, which translates as a command, not simply a feeling or one of many options. We choose to obey and forgive, and our emotions will follow the realization of truth in our hearts.

If a person forgives and he or she still has pain from the event, the pain could be a signal of two things: Something else in that event needs to be forgiven, or another type of sinful response needs to be taken care of (anger, bitterness, etc.). When we forgive, we forgive in faith, believing that the Lord will complete the work. We may not feel different instantly, but our emotions will follow the confession we made in faith.

Releasing the Spiritual Debt

When someone sins against us, it causes a debt in the spiritual realm.[5] Suddenly, we have a debt in our hands, and we have to decide what we are going to do with it.

> "Whenever you stand praying, forgive, if you **have anything against anyone**, so that your Father who is in heaven will also forgive you your transgressions."
> — Mark 11:25, (emphasis added)

The Greek word for have in this passage is echo, which literally means "to hold." Unforgiveness paints a picture of a person holding in his or her hands a piece of paper containing the debt of sin. The problem is that whoever holds the debt has to pay the debt! When Jesus held our sin, He had to pay for the sin.

When we forgive someone, we release that debt of sin. Jesus already paid the debt for all sin, so it actually is an offense against Him to hold the debt of unforgiveness.

Forgiveness Is a Heart Issue

The choice to release an offense must be an act from the heart.[3] Forgiving someone of a past offense cannot be a religious act — a ritual or step we take that does not require the participation of our hearts. It must be a choice from the depths of who we are, from our core.

Confessing the Forgiveness

There is power in our words.[6] Death and life are in the power of the tongue. Words are so powerful that we are saved when we confess who Jesus is: *"With the mouth he confesses, resulting in salvation"* (Romans 10:10). If we confess our sin, our sins are forgiven. God is faithful and righteous to forgive us and cleanse us from all unrighteousness.[7] Unforgiveness is a sin that needs to be forgiven. I encourage people to speak their confessions of forgiveness because it releases the salvation of God in their lives — His refreshing, His life, His strength, His resource.

If, after praying about forgiveness, we still feel emotions associated with the event, it could be a stored emotion — that is, what we are feeling now is the same emotion we were feeling when the event occurred. Negative stored emotions need to be healed; otherwise, we will simply stuff them down into the soul.

We discern whether the emotion is coming from a belief or is a stored emotion through a process of elimination. First, we attempt to free ourselves of the conclusions we came to after the painful event occurred. Second, we deal with any issues of forgiveness that arise. If, after we deal with the conclusions and corresponding forgiveness issues, we still struggle with the painful emotions, we can conclude they are stored emotions.

The Anchor of Our Souls

"This hope we have as an anchor of the soul, a hope both sure and steadfast and one which enters within the veil."
— Hebrews 6:19

A few years ago, I prayed with a young man who was wrestling with homosexuality. We prayed through a significant number of strongholds in his life, and he found freedom from homosexual temptations.

But some time after that, he and I were in the car together, and he confessed, "Rick, recently I've really been dealing with homosexual thoughts. My mind is flooding with thoughts and temptations."

I prayed about it, and the Lord put the answer on my heart. I asked this man, "When's the last time you had a quiet time?"

He answered, "Well, maybe about two, three weeks?"

That was his problem.

Romans 8:5 says, *"For those who are according to the flesh set their minds on the things of the flesh, but those who are according to the Spirit, the things of the Spirit."* If your mind is set on the flesh, you are going to do the deeds of the flesh. If your mind is set on the Spirit, you are going to do the deeds of the Spirit. This young man had not made any choices to set his mind on the Spirit. So of course, he was dealing with issues of the flesh. They were trying to become evident in his life.[8]

Our souls need stability. They constantly seek to attach themselves to someone, someplace, or something that will serve as an anchor. When our hearts are "anchored" to a person, place, or thing, we have established that person, place, or thing as a source of life. The anchor of our souls determines the lasting stability we experience.

In 1 Timothy 6:17, Paul writes, *"Instruct those who are rich in this present world not to be conceited or to fix their hope on the uncertainty of riches, but on God, who richly supplies us with all things to enjoy."* If our hope is attached to the riches of this world—that is, anything other than Jesus—our hope is or will be unstable at some point in time. But a hope fixed on the Lord is firm, lasting, and unshakeable. The answer to the soul's seeking is to attach the hope of our hearts to God's nature and character.

When we "set our minds" on the flesh, we will walk according to the flesh and live out of the flesh's resources and guidance. When we focus our minds on God, we will walk according to the Holy Spirit and live out of His resources and guidance. The Holy Spirit is one with our spirits,[9] so when our souls are focused on, or attached to, the conduit of our spirits, the Holy Spirit's resources and guidance are released into us.

According to Romans 8:4–6, we can discern which conduit we are using through specific emotions. If I stuck my finger in an electrical outlet, my body would receive a jolt of electricity. My body itself would not be generating the electricity; it merely would be serving as a conduit for the electricity. My body feels what passes through it. The soul reacts in a similar way. It is like a sponge—it absorbs whatever it comes in contact with. There are at least three conduits that the soul can attach itself to: the flesh, the spirit, or the soul itself (self-reliance). Each of the conduits will have distinct emotions associated with it, so through our feelings, we can tell where our souls are anchored.

Attached to the Spirit

If the Lord, who is a spiritual Being, is the hope of our souls, our souls are stable. When our souls are anchored to Him as our hope, we experience spiritual emotions:

"The mind set on the Spirit is life and peace."
— Romans 8:6, (emphasis added)

"The fruit of the Spirit is love, joy, peace, patience, kindness, goodness, faithfulness, gentleness, self-control; against such things there is no law."
— Galatians 5:22–23

"The wisdom from above [the Spirit] is first pure, then peaceable, gentle, reasonable, full of mercy and good fruits, unwavering, without hypocrisy. And the seed whose fruit is righteousness is sown in peace by those who make peace."
— James 3:17–18

The human spirit is connected to the Holy Spirit if the person is born again. When our spirits are "one" with the Holy Spirit, we will be able to receive freely all the things given to us by God.[10] A number of emotions signal life in the spirit. For one, we can experience joy:

*"For our heart rejoices in Him,
Because we trust in [attach ourselves to] His holy name."*
— Psalm 33:21

"Now may the God of hope fill you with all joy and peace in believing, so that you will abound in hope by the power of the Holy Spirit."
— Romans 15:13

The soulish emotion of joy is different than happiness. Happiness is the result of "good happenings." If our happenings are good, we are happy, but if our happenings are bad, we are unhappy. Joy supersedes our happenings, both good and bad, because our focus is not on our happenings but on the Lord. The preceding passages of Scripture tell us that we can use the spiritual emotion of joy as a gauge for determining the state of our relationship with God. Joy is the spiritual emotion released in our souls when we are in a state of faith. Notice how the psalmist declared that his heart (the soul) was rejoicing because he trusted the Lord.

When our souls are anchored to the Lord, we also experience peace. Peace is a spiritual emotion that signals we are in right relationship with God:

> *"Glory to God in the highest, And on earth peace among men with whom He is pleased."* — Luke 2:14

> *"The steadfast of mind You will keep in perfect peace, Because he trusts in You."* — Isaiah 26:3

Peace is also a signal we are in right relationship with the people around us: *"If possible, so far as it depends on you, be at peace with all men"* (Romans 12:18). Everyone knows the feeling of "unsettledness" that comes when there is something between us and a brother or sister. If we see our brothers and sisters and it feels like we swallowed a rock, it is a sign that our relationships with those people are not right. But if we see them and feel peace, it is a sign that things are good and right between us.

Attached to the Flesh

Several years ago, a man came to me and said, "Rick, I really need you to pray for me. I'm dealing with a spirit of lust."

In those days, I was ready to cast a demon out of anything—a bush, a rock, anything. So I obliged him. I started praying hard: "In the name of Jesus, I command the spirit of lust to be gone!"

All of a sudden, the Spirit of God spoke to me: "If you cast out his problem, you'll kill him."

The words shocked me. "What do You mean it will kill him?"

The Lord answered, "He does not have an evil spirit. His problem is the flesh."

The man's soul was anchored in his flesh. So I showed him how to deal with the flesh, and he in turn was able to deal with the issue.

If our souls are attached to the Holy Spirit, we are able to feel the emotions of the Spirit within us. But if our souls are not connected to the Spirit, they will easily become attached to the flesh, and the feelings and actions of the flesh will become evident within us.

> "Now the deeds of the flesh are evident, which are: immorality, impurity, sensuality, idolatry, sorcery, enmities, strife, jealousy, outbursts of anger, disputes, dissensions, factions, envying, drunkenness, carousing, and things like these, of which I forewarn you, just as I have forewarned you, that those who practice such things will not inherit the kingdom of God."   — Galatians 5:19–21

When our minds are attached to, or focused on, our flesh, we display distinct and noticeable characteristics. In addition to the emotions listed in Galatians 5:19–21, each of us has unique fleshly signals that our souls can sense. It is important for us to know these signals so we can take action. The other day, I was driving my car and I noticed that an indicator light on my instrument panel was on — one of the tires was underinflated. So I pulled into my mechanic's shop and found out that a screw was stuck in my tire. Without that indictor light, I could have ended up with a flat on the side of the road. If we can recognize our fleshly signals, we can save ourselves a lot of pain.

Our flesh is connected to the world,[11] and the world is attached to and under the devil's authority.[12] If the soul is attached, and therefore open, to the world through the flesh, it is vulnerable to all the things of the world and of the devil.[13] That vulnerability can be a doorway to all kinds of sinful activity.

When I get too busy and do not take the time to set my mind and heart on the Lord, I can easily fall back into sinful flesh patterns. One time, I was frustrated because I kept struggling with lustful thoughts, but as I prayed about it, the Lord revealed to me that I simply had gotten too busy and was not spending time with Him. I corrected my lifestyle and returned to setting my heart and mind on the Lord, and my thoughts righted themselves.

The mind and heart set on the flesh generate the emotions of fleshly lust. The "lust of the flesh" can be very deceiving and seductive. Each of us needs to be aware of what our fleshly lust feels like, so we can recognize what is going on and make the necessary adjustments in the focus of our minds.

Attached to the Soul

If the soul is attached to itself (self-reliance), we will feel jealousy, selfish ambition, and disorder. People who have anchored themselves to themselves believe they can live and advance through intellectual means — they seek to gain victory over the flesh solely through efforts of self-discipline and education.

> "Who among you is wise and understanding? Let him show by his good behavior his deeds in the gentleness of wisdom. But if you have bitter jealousy and selfish ambition in your heart, do not be arrogant and so lie against the truth. This wisdom is not that which comes down from above, but is earthly, natural, demonic. For where jealousy and selfish ambition exist, there is disorder and every evil thing."
> — James 3:13–16

In this passage, we see three negative sources of wisdom: earthly, natural (literally soulish), and demonic. When our souls are anchored to themselves, we are trusting in ourselves, which is a soulish wisdom.

Our souls were not made to be independent of God. When we are not dependent on Him and are anchored to ourselves instead, we are operating out of pride. Using soulish wisdom within a group of people produces disorder (confusion) and "every evil thing," as James says.

Hopelessness: When the Soul is Not Anchored to Anything

"So I say, 'My strength has perished,
And so has my hope from the Lord.'"
— Lamentations 3:18

If nothing serves as an anchor for our souls, we feel hopeless. The emotions of hopelessness and uncertainty can cause a broad spectrum of other emotions, such as fear, panic, and anxiety. In a state of hopelessness, we have no peace, happiness, or strength, and we can end up in depression.

A number of years ago, I made an investment with someone. It was a significant amount of money, and this person stole it. As a result, Paula and I had to sell our house, and I began entertaining thoughts that I was a failure, that I didn't measure up, and that I caused pain and sorrow for my family. There was a time when depression weighed so heavily on me that I would wake up in the morning and feel lower than a snail's belly.

I learned that I needed to get out of bed each morning and boldly confess the truth of God's Word, specifically 2 Corinthians 2:14: *"But thanks be to God, who always leads us in triumph in Christ, and manifests through us the sweet aroma of the knowledge of Him in every place."* I had to declare into my heart and soul the truth that I was not a failure. As I did this, the depression and weight lifted off of me.

It is such a beautiful thing that our heavenly Father would create us with the capacity to feel the thoughts and conclusions of our souls. We can know what kind of conclusions or beliefs are within us before we have a chance to act them out. When we understand soulish emotions, we can change the lies our hearts and minds may be embracing, or we can express the truth our hearts have received from God — and become even more impressionable to God's goodness and love.

137

Key Points of Chapter 6

What is the soulish emotion signaling in our hearts? It could be one of three things:

1. A belief or conclusion in our hearts,
2. A stored emotion from a past event, or
3. The source of our souls (what we are "anchored to").

Most of the time, we feel soulish emotions because of the way our beliefs are interpreting a particular environment or event. The best way we can determine if the soulish emotion is coming from a belief in our hearts or from a momentary focus of the mind is to evaluate the thoughts we were thinking before and during the emotion.

When we are able to deal with the beliefs that hinder us, we are no longer subject to the devil's schemes, tossed around emotionally and swamped with feelings of instability.

It is important for us to differentiate the signals of our emotions so we can take the next step and respond to those emotions. We will talk about responding to our emotions in the next two chapters.

Notes / Reference Scriptures

[A] For more information about these tools, visit www.dealingjesus.org.

1. John 14:30
2. 2 Corinthians 2:10-11
3. Matthew 18:32-35
4. Matthew 6:12; Luke 6:37-38
5. Matthew 6:12
6. Proverbs 18:21
7. 1 John 1:9
8. Galatians 5:19
9. 1 Corinthians 6:17
10. 1 Corinthians 2:9-12
11. 1 John 2:16
12. John 12:31
13. Ephesians 2:1-3; 1 John 5:19

Responding to Soulish Emotions Part 1: Truth-Based Emotions

*"For since the creation of the world His invisible attributes, His eternal power and divine nature, have been clearly seen, being understood through what has been made, so that they are without excuse. For even though they knew God, they did **not honor [glorify] Him as God or give thanks**, but they became futile in their speculations, and their foolish heart was darkened."*
— Romans 1:20–21, (emphasis added)

In Romans 1, Paul talks about people who have revelation from God, but they do not glorify Him as God or have hearts of thanksgiving. Because of this, they become desensitized to Him: "Their foolish heart was darkened."

If we feel a soulish emotion and do not respond to it, we will eventually lose the capability of feeling that emotion. When our hearts and minds deem something unimportant, we close off our ability to hear and feel it. It is similar to living near an airport or railroad track; we become desensitized to the sounds of planes and trains, and eventually, we no longer notice them. God created us to respond to soulish emotions. Whether the emotion is signaling a truth or a lie, it is important we respond to it in some manner.

Responding to physical emotions can be fairly simple. If

I have a headache, I can pray, believe God for healing, and possibly take some pain medication. Responding to soulish emotions, however, is a little more complex. Our response to soulish emotions can bring sensitivity or insensitivity, revelation or deadness of heart, life or death. Remember that soulish emotions reveal conclusions or beliefs that have been established in our hearts. They can also be the stored emotions from past events or can signal the current focus of our minds—what our minds are "attached to."

Responding to soulish emotions can involve a number of different actions, but first, we need to know what we are feeling. Are we angry? Are we frustrated? Are we lonely? After we have determined the nature of the soulish emotion, we need to apply the foundations of God's truth so we can discern what is truth and what is a lie despite what we are feeling.

When I was a boy, I had a friend who almost died from a ruptured appendix because the doctors misread his body's signals. They didn't realize what was happening inside him. Along the same lines, we can shut ourselves down emotionally and lose that ability to feel and receive revelation. We always need to respond to soulish emotions in some manner. Our response depends on what they are signaling.

Responding to Truth-Based Emotions

Our response to an emotional signal of truth differs from our response to an emotion that is signaling a lie. With a truth-based emotion, we need to appropriately express that emotion; with a lie-based emotion, we need to get to the root of it and change the emotion. An emotion signaling a truth can be a feeling like joy or love, but it can also be a feeling like sorrow or grief. Both types of emotion can be based on truth and need to be expressed.

If the emotion is based on truth, we need to express that emotion in a positive manner. We do this so we will not become hardened and take for granted the good things God has given us. Jesus spoke about this in Luke 8:18: *"So take care how you listen; for whoever has, to him more shall be given; and whoever does not have, even what he thinks he has shall be taken away from him."* When we take care to "listen" to soulish emotions that signal truth, we can hear even more truth and not lose touch with the truth that is already valued and sacred to us.

When we respond to positive soulish emotions, three things occur:

1. We establish spiritual emotions like love and joy in our hearts (this occurs when we respond to a truth we are hearing for the first time).
2. We maintain and keep the treasures of truth already established in our hearts.
3. We become more impressionable and more readily able to receive the truth of God.[1]

When I see my wife, Paula, my soul is filled with joy and love for her. It is important that I express these emotions to her so my love for her will grow. If I see her and I do not respond to my emotions, my lack of response can easily cause my love to start to wane.

Processing Grief and Sorrow

Sorrow and grief are a part of life. When Lazarus died, Jesus wept alongside Mary and Martha. He expressed His grief, but He did not allow the sorrow to distract Him from carrying out the will and heart of His Father.

In Psalm 42, the psalmist expressed his grief at being separated from his homeland. Notice the painful longing he had for the Lord and his country:

"Why are you in despair, O my soul?
And why have you become disturbed within me?
Hope in God, for I shall again praise Him
For the help of His presence.
O my God, my soul is in despair within me;
Therefore I remember You from the land of the Jordan
And the peaks of Hermon, from Mount Mizar."

— Psalm 42:5–6

The saints in the Old Covenant weren't able to sense the presence of God all the time as we can today. In most situations, they experienced His presence only with the multitude and in the temple. In this psalm, the writer missed the Promised Land, and it caused him to feel despair. He longed for the days when he had experienced the Lord in his homeland. The important detail here is that he expressed the longing of his soul. He did not stuff the emotion.

When Jesus was heartbroken over the hardness of the religious leaders of His day, He responded by verbalizing His passion for His people. He did not try to hide the emotion or shut it down—He responded by appropriately expressing it:

"Jerusalem, Jerusalem, who kills the prophets and stones those who are sent to her! How often I wanted to gather your children together, the way a hen gathers her chicks under her wings, and you were unwilling. Behold, your house is being left to you desolate! For I say to you, from now on you will not see Me until you say, 'Blessed is He who comes in the name of the Lord!'"

— Matthew 23:37–39

As we talked about in an earlier chapter, when Jesus was angry with the Pharisees, He responded to His anger by healing instead of causing destruction:

"After looking around at them with anger, grieved at their hardness of heart, He said to the man, 'Stretch out your hand.' And he stretched it out, and his hand was restored."

— Mark 3:5

In this situation, the Pharisees were revealing a lie in their hearts. It both angered and grieved Jesus, and He responded to His emotion in a proper manner. Just because we feel a negative soulish emotion does not mean we should express that same emotion. If we feel anger, for example, we do not have to respond in anger. Sometimes the best response to a negative soulish emotion is simply to acknowledge it in a safe manner.

When my mother was dying, fear and sorrow tried to push me into unbelief. She had been sick with a debilitating disease for a number of years and had been hospitalized only for some simple tests, but she developed pneumonia. My dad called me and told me to come because Mom had taken a turn for the worse. When I walked into my mother's room, I could hear her fighting to breathe.

I couldn't take it. As I listened to her struggle, my soul was swamped with pain and sorrow. Running out into the woods behind the hospital, I screamed and cried out to God, begging Him to keep my mom from suffering. I knew she wanted to go and be with her Savior in Heaven; I was able to handle that truth, but I could not take seeing and hearing her suffer. I responded to the grief and sorrow by expressing it to my heavenly Father.

I got my courage back up and returned to the room to sit by my mother's bed, holding her hand. I listened as she tried to fill her lungs and quote God's promises, and I prayed the same prayer I had prayed out behind the hospital. Grief and sorrow dominated me as I quietly expressed my heart to my Father.

It was in those moments when the Lord declared a truth that anchored me. It was so strong a revelation that I could almost audibly hear it. He said, "Rick, I know how you feel. In the same way and for the same reason, I watched My Son suffer. It is because of sin." I knew He didn't mean my mother had sinned, but it was the condition of sin in the world that was causing this death.[2]

When the Lord spoke to me, the painful grief and sorrow in my soul lifted, and the peace that surpasses all of my understanding filled me. Later that night, when Mom went home to be with the Lord, I was able to face those moments with hope. If I had not responded to the pain of my mother's sickness by respectfully expressing my heart to the Lord, the pain of that event could have caused a destructive form of bitterness in my soul.

When we stuff emotions like grief and sorrow, we cause parts of our hearts to shut down. Emotions like grief and sorrow need to be expressed and processed properly. Ministers constantly deal with pain and sorrow in other people's lives, and I see a lot of them end up shutting their hearts down because they do not properly process this flow of pain and suffering. One professional psychologist I knew stopped attending to the emotions he experienced while counseling others, and he eventually turned to alcohol to dull the ache of dealing with others' pain and suffering every day.

It may not be very professional, but many times as I am counseling others, I will weep as I hear and see the effects of pain and sorrow in their lives. I believe the Lord allows me to weep like that so my heart does not become hardened to the effects of sin and death in the world.

Processing Joy and Love

Just as it is important to express our sorrow and grief, it is also important to express joy and love. We need to respond appropriately to these emotions as well.

We cannot have a revelation of God without having some type of emotion:

> *"Rejoice in the Lord always; again I will say, rejoice!"*
> — Philippians 4:4

> *"Then when he arrived and **witnessed the grace of God, he rejoiced** and began to encourage them all with resolute heart to remain true to the Lord."*
> — Acts 11:23, (emphasis added)

*"The precepts of the Lord are right, **rejoicing the heart**;*
The commandment of the Lord is pure, enlightening the
eyes."   — Psalm 19:8, (emphasis added)

"I have set the Lord continually before me;
Because He is at my right hand, I will not be shaken.
*Therefore **my heart is glad** and my glory rejoices;*
My flesh also will dwell securely."
                      — Psalm 16:8–9, (emphasis added)

*"Therefore you too have grief now; but **I will see you***
***again, and your heart will rejoice**, and no one will take*
your joy away from you."
                      — John 16:22, (emphasis added)

These are just a few of the passages that illustrate the correlation between the revelation of God and our emotions. As we respond to His revelations, we become more impressionable toward Him. In fact, the Lord encourages us to respond emotionally to Him. He wants our hearts to overflow with love for Him. When we experience emotions like love and joy and we respond to them in a positive manner, we become more sensitive to the things of God.

Responding to revelations of God's character and nature is crucial to our walk with Him. That is why the Psalms contain more than fifty different expressions of praise, thanksgiving, and worship. When we respond to God's greatness, we honor Him, and we also empower our hearts to receive even greater revelations of Him.

God's Word often mentions love in the imperative, or command, mode. Why? Because the emotion of love must be expressed in order to bring about its fullness. For example, John writes in 1 John 3:17, **"Whoever has the world's goods, and sees his brother in need and closes his heart against him, how does the love of God abide in him?"** If we see someone in need but do not respond in love, the love of God is not brought into fullness in our lives. We need to respond to what we feel.

So in summary, if the soulish emotion is based on truth,

we need to respond to the emotion by expressing it in some manner. A soulish emotion based on truth can either be a positive, joyous emotion or a grievous emotion. If it is grievous and we do not appropriately respond, our hearts can easily become hardened and callous. If the emotion is joyous and we do not respond, it can hinder us from receiving greater revelations of God's best for us.

The Past: Is It Nostalgia or Inspiration?

I travel a lot, and in the early days, I would be gone for more than three weeks at a time. When you're gone for that length of time, you really have to guard your heart so you don't start to entertain thoughts of home and direct your focus away from what God is doing right in front of you.

One time I took an extended ministry trip overseas, and I began to feel nostalgic about my home. One thing I did to transition my emotions was to listen to a worship song that was very special to me. A dear friend had written it, and my son had made the video for it, so both aspects of the song were precious to me. I would listen to this song of the past, but instead of thinking about the past, I would worship God right where I was, in the present. My heart would be strengthened in the Lord, who is God of the past, present, and future.

When we consider positive soulish emotions, we need to be aware of something I call the "nostalgia effect." We all know the feeling that can fill our souls when we start thinking about the "good ole days." Emotions of nostalgia come out of conclusions based on fondly remembered times. Obviously, positive memories are good things. They are treasures for our hearts to cherish; however, they are not to be used as a driving force for the present and the future. Numerous divorces and affairs occur because of the nostalgia effect. The emotions from past relationships can become so strong that people act on them.

A man once told Jesus that he would follow Him, but first, he had to go and tell his loved ones goodbye. Jesus said to him, *"No one, after putting his hand to the plow and looking back, is fit for the kingdom of God"* (Luke 9:62). God is always doing something new. I once heard Graham Cooke say, *"We cannot find security in what God does. We can only find security in who God is. The reason why we cannot find security in what God does is because God is always doing the impossible."*

The time Jesus spent on earth was affected by the religious leaders' infatuation with the past. It seems like they were always bringing up Abraham, Isaac, Jacob, Moses, David, and the past prophets. They were so enamored with their religious history that they were not able to embrace the phenomenal present relationship with God. He was being manifested in their midst in the flesh.

In a similar way, many Christians talk about the good ole days. Entire denominations will use something only if it is old, believing that documents, practices, and beliefs from a certain period of time are more significant than those of the present. However, the present days are the "good days" as well — they simply are not "old" yet. We use the past to build our faith for the uncertainties of the present and the future, but that is all. God is always working forward — to cause all things to work out for our good.[3]

The nostalgia effect can hinder us in three ways. First, it hinders our hearts from being able to live by faith. Faith is *"the conviction of things not seen"* (Hebrews 11:1). A life of faith is a life in the unknown. We know the past. We know what to expect back there. The nostalgia effect makes the life of faith look difficult and unsafe.

The children of Israel fell prey to the nostalgia effect, and it hindered them from going forward and receiving God's best:

> *"Our fathers were unwilling to be obedient to him, but repudiated him and in their hearts turned back to Egypt."*
> — Acts 7:39

"They refused to listen,
And did not remember Your wondrous deeds which You
had performed among them;
So they became stubborn and appointed a leader to return
to their slavery in Egypt.
But You are a God of forgiveness,
Gracious and compassionate,
Slow to anger and abounding in lovingkindness;
And You did not forsake them."

— Nehemiah 9:17

When the Hebrews came out of Egypt, they encountered seasons of wilderness, during which various temptations hit their hearts. As they struggled with a lack of water, the known past-life of slavery and abuse seemed much more secure than the life of freedom found in the unknown present and future. God miraculously provided for them every day, with a manna that was totally unfamiliar to them,[4] but because of the uncertainty of the wilderness, they longed for the familiar; they wanted what they had eaten in Egypt.[5] Instead of allowing the Lord to be their security through faith, they wanted the familiar past to be their security.

Second, the nostalgia effect causes us to be unable to embrace the present and future. It hinders us because we are using the past as the standard with which to evaluate what is happening now and where we are going:

"The sons of Israel said to them, 'Would that we had died
by the Lord's hand in the land of Egypt, when we sat by
the pots of meat, when we ate bread to the full; for you
have brought us out into this wilderness to kill this whole
assembly with hunger.'" — Exodus 16:3

Finally, the nostalgia effect seen in Exodus 16 glamourized the past and made it seem better than it really was. The children of Israel had been slaves in Egypt! The Egyptians had treated them harshly. Yet we see the Hebrews thinking about Egypt as if it were the Promised Land. The nostalgia effect kept them from finding their comfort and peace in the Lord.

God wants our memories of the past to be an inspiration to believe in the present. The Lord is our hope and future, and we need to be ready to partner with Him no matter what He is doing. God calls us to remember the past—not to encourage us to go back to it but to enable us to embrace the future:

> "Remember those who led you, who spoke the word of God to you; and considering the result of their conduct, imitate their faith. Jesus Christ is the same yesterday and today and forever."   — Hebrews 13:7–8

The Lord is the God of the past, the present, and the future. That is why we can use the past to inspire our faith for the future, even though that future remains unseen.

In Joshua 4:6–7, God told the people of Israel:

> "Let this be a sign among you, so that when your children ask later, saying, 'What do these stones mean to you?' then you shall say to them, 'Because the waters of the Jordan were cut off before the ark of the covenant of the Lord; when it crossed the Jordan, the waters of the Jordan were cut off.' So these stones shall become a memorial to the sons of Israel forever."

God had His people set up reminders of what He had done for them in the past—to inspire them to look forward to what He would do for their children. When I was in college, God led a group of us to put on a series of concerts. The first concert cost $660. This was a whole lot of money for college students back in the '70s, but we believed God for it, and He provided the money for us.

A few months later, we were praying again, and we felt the Lord tell us, "I want you to do another concert." He even told us which artists to invite—artists who were really popular in those days. One man alone cost $9,000 to book.

We decided, "Okay. Let's believe God for it! Let's start this process."

A week or two later, God told us another artist to invite. This one cost $6,500. So now our concert was going to cost $15,500 just for the artists, and the sound and lighting would cost another $1,000. Because we had believed God for $660, we were able to say, "Okay, God—You did it for $660. You can do it for $16,500." We were looking back to believe God for what He could do in the present.

Years later, another group of us experienced a similar thing when we bought our church building. We had $4,000 in the bank account, and the building was listed for $1.2 million. Because of what God had done in the past, when we saw that obstacle, we were able to look forward and believe for what He could do in the present and in the future.

> *"Remember His wonders which He has done,*
> *His marvels and the judgments uttered by His mouth."*
> — Psalm 105:5

> *"I shall remember the deeds of the Lord;*
> *Surely I will remember Your wonders of old."*
> — Psalm 77:11

Key Points of Chapter 7

It is very important to respond to what we are feeling, even if the soulish emotion is signaling a lie.

Responding to soulish emotions can involve a number of different actions, but first, we need to know what we are feeling (anger, frustration, fear, etc.). Then after we have determined the nature of the soulish emotion, we need to lay the foundations of God's truth so we can know what is truth and what is a lie despite what we are feeling.

Responding to Truth-Based Emotions

If the emotion is based on truth, we need to express that emotion in a positive manner. We do this so we will not become hardened and take for granted the good things God has given us.

When we respond to positive soulish emotions, three things occur:

1. We establish spiritual emotions like love and joy in our hearts (this occurs when we respond to a truth we are hearing for the first time).
2. We maintain and keep the treasures of truth already established in our hearts.
3. We become more impressionable and more readily able to receive the truth of God.[1]

Notes / Reference Scriptures

1. Hebrews 5:14
2. Romans 5:12
3. Romans 8:28
4. Deuteronomy 8:16
5. Numbers 11:5-6

Responding to Soulish Emotions Part 2: Lie-Based Emotions

For me, the exciting thing about negative soulish emotions is that if we understand and recognize the signals, they can be an easy way to identify where our hearts are anchored. We can then refocus ourselves on the Spirit, or deal with the issues in our hearts that are causing our minds to focus on the flesh.

Several times through the years when Paula and I have entered a "discussion," she will look at me and say, "Rick, you need to go have a quiet time."

Because my soul was anchored in the flesh, negative emotions like anger and impatience were coming out of me, and she was catching them head on. But she has recognized that if I put myself in the presence of God, I can get back into the Spirit and then come and love her with Jesus' love.

Whenever soulish emotions that signal a lie arise in our hearts, God's desire is that our first response would be in line with the character and nature of who He is. We do not want to express or act out an emotion that is not in line with His truth. If we act or speak out a lie, it can lead to further bondage. For example, if someone wrongs me, and I feel anger in my heart and speak or act in a manner to hurt that person, it gives the devil a place in my life.[1] Remember that in Mark 3:5,

Jesus was angry with the Pharisees, but He healed instead of causing destruction. His response brought life, not pain or retribution.[2] So the first thing we want to keep in mind with lie-based emotions is not to speak, think, or act out of anything that is not in line with God's truth.

Just as we want to value soulish emotions that signal truth, we also want to value soulish emotions that signal lies. If the emotion signals a conclusion that does not line up with God's nature and character, we now have the opportunity to change the conclusion. If we didn't feel that emotion, we wouldn't have any way of knowing what was present in our hearts until it was too late—we would be speaking or acting out the lie and further establishing it within us. Instead of employing the emotion, we want to change the conclusion being signaled.

I often watch people try to suppress or deny the ungodly emotions that are signaling lies in their hearts. However, instead of ignoring the emotion, we want to allow the Holy Spirit to reveal the lies signaled by the emotion. When we simply rebuke or try to ignore the emotion, we are attempting to clean the "outside" of our lives without dealing with the inside. Jesus rebuked the Pharisees for being more concerned with outward appearances than with issues of the heart.[3] We do not want to deny what we are feeling; we want to allow the Lord to change the conclusions being signaled by the emotion. When we respond appropriately to ungodly emotions, it can lead to freedom and life. Telling ourselves, "Don't feel that way," doesn't do anything of worth—it is simply cleaning the outside of the "cup and dish." We want to clean our hearts so the reality of freedom is brought forth.

One night at a Bible study, I was teaching about the reality of ministry and how you sometimes have to deal with ugly, painful things. I went deep into the gory details of some hardcore ministry situations.

My wife said to me quietly, "Too many details."

It pushed my buttons, and impatience rose up inside me. In a very harsh, firm voice, I told her, "I want them to know the details!" I then went on teaching as if nothing had happened.

After the study as Paula and I walked out to our car, I was feeling pretty good about how the evening had gone. But as soon as we got into the car, Paula gently said to me, "I want you to know that you hurt me tonight."

I sat there speechless and finally asked, "How did I hurt you?"

She proceeded to talk about the situation I just related. I felt anger rise up in my heart, along with a strong temptation to defend myself, but the Lord lovingly told me to hush up and listen. He brought to mind 1 Corinthians 13:5 — love is not provoked. The Lord revealed to me that I had left love. When Paula interrupted me during my teaching, I did not respond in love to her. Instead, my heart had been provoked, and in my response, I had left the Spirit and turned to the flesh. The Lord further revealed to me that Paula's words during the meeting had uncovered two strongholds in my heart. So right then, I started dealing with the strongholds, and my heart was set free in those areas.

The negative emotions that cropped up in my soul revealed to me a set of lies in my heart. Remember that we do not want to express the emotions that come from lies — we do not want to become more sensitive to sin. Instead, we want to respond to these emotions by asking the Lord to reveal their root. What lie is the emotion signaling? When we know the root of the lie, we can deal with it.

Certain negative soulish emotions can be deceiving because they feel "pleasant" but contain a negative end result. They are destructive. For example, if a man entertains sexual lust in his mind, it will "feel good" to him, but eventually it will push him to take physical action. The end result of that emotion will be some type of death. The old '70s saying, "If it feels good, do it!" is not always a statement that brings life.

The world often says, "If you feel something, you need to express it. Whatever it is, just express it." But that can get us killed. As believers, we want to take these steps every time we feel something:

1. We identify whether or not the emotion is a soulish emotion.
2. We identify if it is a positive or negative emotion.
3. If it is negative, we respond in a way that brings healing and life.
4. If it is positive, we respond in a manner that accentuates the emotion and makes us more impressionable.

Various forms of depression, hopelessness, fear, and similar emotions reveal we have made conclusions that are not based in God's truth. Negative soulish emotions can be feelings of pain that reference specific upsetting, or traumatic, events of the past. These painful emotions can push us into fear and doubt and cause us to erect walls toward others and God. Whenever these soulish emotions arise in our hearts, God's desire is for us to alter those emotions.

Bring Your Emotions into the Light

The first step in processing a soulish emotion that reveals a lie is to bring the emotion into the light.

> *"But all things become visible when they are exposed by the light, for everything that becomes visible is light."*
> — Ephesians 5:13

There are a number of ways we bring our emotions "into the light" in order to discern the root of what we are feeling. The main way to discern an emotion's source is to ask the Lord. David prayed in Psalm 17:2, *"Let my judgment come forth from Your presence."* The light of God's presence is a very powerful force in regard to what we are feeling and seeing. It brings clarity.

Second, we can bring our emotions into the light by "judging" them with the Word of God. If I feel a love of money or a desire to get rich, I know that emotion is going to lead me to temptation and trouble.[4]

Sometimes our thoughts and emotions can be in such turmoil that it is hard to see what is true. In these times, it is good to seek others' help. My wife and other people in the Body of Christ are good sources to help me discern the truth when I am overwhelmed. Praying with others helps us get in God's presence and see things much more clearly.

For example, I once returned home from a two-week overseas ministry trip on a Monday. I had contracted a cold toward the end of the trip, and I was not feeling well when I arrived home. I was scheduled to preach on the following Sunday. Tullio, one of our church leaders, asked me if I should preach or not, but I was so tired and sick that I could not discern clearly. I also felt guilty for having been gone for two weeks and didn't want to let people down. So in the midst of all of these physical and soulish emotions, I resisted Tullio's counsel and pressed forward and preached. The results were disastrous! If I had listened to Tullio's counsel in sorting out what I was feeling, I could have saved myself from a good deal of embarrassment.

When we bring a lie-based soulish emotion into the light, we can discern its source. Have you ever tried to find something in a pitch-black room? I have to feel around and constantly evaluate what I touch, but when I turn the lights on, it is easy to find what I am looking for. One early morning, I was getting ready for work while Paula was still asleep. The darkness in the room made it difficult for me to pick out my clothes. When I got to work, I realized I had put on two different-colored socks. I was embarrassed several times that day as I tried to explain the reason for my colorful socks! God is very faithful to reveal what needs to be revealed in our hearts. In His light, we can see clearly.

Redeeming the Soulish Emotion

A lie-based soulish emotion could be signaling the current focus of our minds. Our minds could be set on the flesh;[5] they could be overcome by our circumstances,[6] or they could be fixated on a lie the devil has conned us into believing. No matter the source, the results and effects are the same, because the devil is the ruler and god of this world,[7] and he wants to draw us into it. Our flesh is "attached" to the world and will reflect the occurrences of the world.[8]

Fleshly lust wages war on the soul.[9] It creates powerful thoughts that seek to entice our souls into becoming focused on the will and needs of the flesh. The emotions generated by fleshly lust can be very enticing and dominating:

> "... whose end is destruction, whose god is their appetite, and whose glory is in their shame, who set their minds on earthly things." — Philippians 3:19

The goal of this type of lie is to make the flesh's appetites our god. If that happens, we will feed our flesh when it is in need, no matter the cost, and we will obey its lust.[10] When we recognize that what we are feeling is a lust of the flesh, it is very important for us not to give way to that emotion. Instead, we need to redirect our minds and hearts toward the Lord and the things of the Spirit.

When we are dealing with fleshly lust, it is not an issue of trying to die to the flesh, because we have already died to the flesh through the cross of Jesus Christ.[11] The issue revolves around how we are living. If we are living to the Lord in the Holy Spirit, we will automatically put to death the deeds and emotions of fleshly lust:

> "If you are living according to the flesh, you must die; but if by the Spirit you are putting to death the deeds of the body, you will live." — Romans 8:13

People who have been set free from an addiction to cigarettes will most likely experience a season in which their flesh attempts to entice them back into smoking. During those times, the emotions of fleshly lust will fill their souls, and the people can almost feel carried toward smoking again. For many, it seems overwhelming, but victory can be achieved in those moments when the emotions of lust are the strongest.

The devil is the ruler of this world. Using the world's adversities, he continually seeks to distract our hearts and minds from the goodness of God and the anchor of His Word. When the intense circumstances of the world swirl over us, it is easy for our thoughts to become fixated on those circumstances. As that happens, our minds can easily become overwhelmed with worries and fears, and if these worries and fears go unchecked, we could be pushed into all kinds of trouble.

> *"Rest in the Lord and wait patiently for Him;*
> *Do not fret because of him who prospers in his way,*
> *Because of the man who carries out wicked schemes.*
> *Cease from anger and forsake wrath;*
> *Do not fret; it leads only to evildoing."*
>
> — Psalm 37:7–8

The adversities of the world can serve as an open door for the enemy to weigh our souls down with negative soulish emotions.[12] He intends to distract us from the sufficiency of our heavenly Father. The best way to face these emotions is to lay foundations of truth. Every one of us will face some type of adversity in this world. The question is whether or not we will prepare for these adversities. I was raised in Florida where hurricanes are a frequent reality. When a hurricane was coming our way, it was very important for us to prepare. If we didn't, it could be devastating. Jesus warns that we will face storms in this life; therefore, we must prepare.

> *"Therefore, let everyone who is godly pray to You in a*
> *time when You may be found;*
> *Surely in a flood of great waters they will not reach him.*
> *You are my hiding place; You preserve me from trouble;*
> *You surround me with songs of deliverance."*
>
> — Psalm 32:6–7

> *"Therefore everyone who hears these words of Mine and*
> *acts on them, may be compared to a wise man who built*
> *his house on the rock. And the rain fell, and the floods*

came, and the winds blew and slammed against that house; and yet it did not fall, for it had been founded on the rock."   — Matthew 7:24–25

Anytime we experience soulish emotions because of difficult current events, we can utilize our foundations in God's truth to evaluate what we are sensing. When we do this, we will not be shaken.[13] Isaiah affirms this principle when he says, *"The steadfast of mind You will keep in perfect peace, because he trusts in You"* (Isaiah 26:3). When we face worrisome and fearful events, focusing our minds and hearts on the character of God brings stability and peace into our lives. The comforting truth is that if we prepare for the storms by allowing the Lord to become our delight and our Source for living, we will overcome adversities.

As we attempt to redirect soulish emotions that signal a current event, the main thing to do is allow the Lord to reveal His truth about the situation. Jesus did this with the disciples when they were experiencing the soulish emotion of fear and abandonment: *"But I tell you the truth, it is to your advantage that I go away; for if I do not go away, the Helper will not come to you; but if I go, I will send Him to you"* (John 16:7). He redirected their minds and hearts toward the revelation of a new truth — the Holy Spirit was about to be sent to them, and they would not be left alone. The Spirit would love on them the same way Jesus did. When they focused on the truth of the situation, they were able to calm their fears.[14]

Jesus continuously directed His emotions toward life.[15] Every negative soulish emotion that signals a current event can be redirected to bring about positive emotions — in other words, the painful things we feel can be altered so they actually bring us peace.

When adversities of the world start to overwhelm me, one of my favorite things to do is declare the Word of God. As I confess the Word, I can sense the Holy Spirit's joy and peace start to fill my soul. I also use the tools of praise and worship. They direct the focus of my mind away from my current circumstances. When I am combating current soulish emotions of worry and doubt, I can strengthen myself in the Lord through prayer.

> *"Be anxious for nothing, but in everything by prayer and supplication with thanksgiving let your requests be made known to God. And the peace of God, which surpasses all comprehension, will guard your hearts and your minds in Christ Jesus."*   — Philippians 4:6–7

When my daughter, Michele, was little, Paula and I noticed an unsightly mole-like bump on her back. We took her to a pediatrician, and he immediately started talking about the possibility of something serious. He said we had to get it taken care of right away and made us an appointment with a surgeon for the following week.

When I got home, I called a surgeon friend of mine and told him the situation, and he wanted us to come to his office the next morning. That night was horrific to my soul. I was tormented with thoughts of something being seriously wrong with my little girl. My only relief came through prayer and the power of God's Word hidden in my soul; I needed to be in the secret place of my Father's presence. His peace and love comforted me. Thanks to the Lord, the bump on Michele's back turned out to be nothing of significance.

The devil continually tries to shoot the fiery darts of his lies into our hearts. He knows that if a lie can take root within us, the emotions of that lie will carry us away into sin and death.[16] If what we are feeling is based on one of his lies, we immediately need to take it captive.[17] I often have random thoughts pop into my mind that I know are sent from the enemy. Once I recognize where the thought comes from, I simply take the thought captive and redirect my thoughts to the Lord and His goodness, love, righteousness, and holiness.

Whenever we recognize that our emotions are coming from a lie, it is important for us to redirect our thoughts back to the Lord and His abundant provisions and love.

Altering Negative Soulish Emotions

If I know my emotion is coming from a lie that I believe to be truth, and I attempt to redirect my thoughts but my thoughts refuse to be redirected, the emotion is most likely coming from a stronghold — or, within our context, a past event. Negative soulish emotions can be the stored emotions of a past event that the enemy is trying to bring up in the present.

Imagine a splinter stuck in a person's hand. If the splinter penetrated the hand with such force that bruising occurred, the area around the splinter would be discolored and tender to the touch. That bruising is the equivalent of stored emotions. The splinter symbolizes the "conclusion" the person reached because of the event. There are two problems: the splinter itself and the bruising. The splinter has to be removed, and the bruising has to heal. In natural circumstances, when the splinter is removed, the body heals itself and the bruising disappears over time, but that is not the case with negative soulish emotions. The splinter may be gone, but the unprocessed negative emotions can affect our hearts and continue to hold us back from the purposes God has for us. A woman who has been through a traumatic sexual event will have to deal with the multi-faceted strongholds that such an event can build. Even though she processes the "splinters" of the event, the emotions of the event will likely need to be healed as well.

It is important that we get to the root lie of an emotion and deal with any strongholds accompanying that lie. "Pulling down" strongholds is critical for complete healing, yet even after a stronghold has been dealt with, sometimes the pain of a broken heart and the emotion of the event still need to be addressed.

Before Peter could be the leader he was destined to be, he had to be healed from the pain of denying Jesus. Peter's actions wounded his own heart. Peter, the rough, tough, confident follower of Jesus, was rendered an uncertain and wondering man. After the resurrection, a series of significant events reveals the pain Peter experienced.

When Peter and John heard that Jesus had been raised from the dead, they ran to the tomb. John saw the empty tomb and believed, but there is no such statement regarding Peter:

> *"And so Simon Peter also came, following him, and entered the tomb; and he saw the linen wrappings lying there . . . So the other disciple who had first come to the tomb then also entered, and he saw and believed. For as yet they did not understand the Scripture, that He must rise again from the dead. So the disciples went away again to their own homes."* — John 20:6–10

The assumption is that Peter did not fully believe Jesus was alive. After that event, Peter and John were not united in faith; they simply went to their own homes, probably confused about what had happened and trying to figure out what to do next.

Later in the chapter, Peter participated in at least three major spiritual events. First, the disciples rejoiced when they saw Jesus in John 20:20. They received the Holy Spirit in John 20:22, and finally, Peter observed Thomas' beautiful experience with the resurrected Jesus, when Thomas saw His wounds and put his full trust in Him. However, despite these events, the pain in Peter's heart hindered him from being able to grasp the fullness of the resurrected Lord.

In John 21, we see Peter going back to what he knew he could do without failing, and that was fishing:

> *"Simon Peter, and Thomas called Didymus, and Nathanael of Cana in Galilee, and the sons of Zebedee, and two others of His disciples were together. Simon Peter said to them, 'I am going fishing.' They said to him, 'We will also come with you.' They went out and got into the boat; and that night they caught nothing."* — John 21:2–3

At this point, Peter was not looking for Jesus. He was simply wandering around wanting to do what was familiar and comfortable to him. The pain of his failure put him in a state of indecision and kept him from understanding the promise of God.

Leaving the disciples there in the boat for a moment, let's look back to the heartbreaking night when Peter denied Jesus. Before the denial, Peter boastfully stated that he was Jesus' man. He more or less declared he would be faithful to Him even unto death. But just a few hours later, Peter denied knowing Him. He didn't do this once but three times. After the third time, Jesus looked at him through the crowd, and Peter remembered the prophetic word Jesus had given him:

> *"But Peter said, 'Man, I do not know what you are talk-ing about.' Immediately, while he was still speaking, a rooster crowed. The Lord turned and looked at Peter. And Peter remembered the word of the Lord, how He had told him, 'Before a rooster crows today, you will deny Me three times.' And he went out and wept bitterly."*
> — Luke 22:60–62

That event had to have been a dagger in Peter's heart. According to Zodhiates, the Greek word for wept means "weep, wail, or lament." Peter's sorrow is described as so deep that his whole body expressed it. Adding to this de-scription, Luke uses the term bitterly. Peter wept bitterly. The addition of that word shows that his intense weeping came from a deep regret and a feeling of failure. Peter was intensely weeping in bitterness and regret. His heart was broken and filled with the emotions of disappointment and failure.

Another interesting dynamic is that this event occurred while Peter and the others were warming themselves over a charcoal fire.[18] Every time he smelled a charcoal fire after that, it likely reminded him of that dreadful night of his denial. Remember that emotions and the sense of smell are two of the strongest imprinters of information on our hearts. We can easily remember events that accompany powerful emotions or strong smells.

With these foundations, we return to the scene where Peter and the other disciples were fishing, attempting to deny the pain of recent events. But even though fishing was their "safe place," that night it failed them — they didn't catch a thing. No doubt, this caused the pain and sense of failure in Peter's heart to do nothing but increase.

Then Jesus showed up. At first, His men did not recognize Him. From the shore, He told them to cast their nets on the other side of the boat, and after they had done so, their catch was so great that they could not haul it in. When the disciples recognized Jesus, Peter threw himself into the water while the others steered the boat to shore, dragging the net filled with fish.

For years, I thought that Peter jumped into the sea to swim to Jesus. But as I read the passage recently, I realized he was most likely tending to the net behind the boat — he was hiding from Jesus, holding on to the pain and the shame of denying Him. When the disciples met Jesus on the shore, He told them to bring some fish, even though He had already started a fire and laid fish and bread upon it:

> *"But the other disciples came in the little boat, for they were not far from the land, but about one hundred yards away, dragging the net full of fish.*
> *So when they got out on the land, they saw a charcoal fire already laid and fish placed on it, and bread. Jesus said to them, 'Bring some of the fish which you have now caught.' Simon Peter went up and drew the net to land, full of large fish, a hundred and fifty-three; and although there were so many, the net was not torn."*
> — John 21:8-11

Notice that Peter "went up" and drew the net to land. He was just coming up out of the sea — at that point, not before. He was focusing on the fish.

Jesus fed them breakfast around a charcoal fire — He used the sense of smell to help redeem Peter's broken heart. Jesus said nothing to him about the denial. Instead, He sought to heal what had been broken. Three times, He asked Peter if Peter loved Him. And three times Peter told Jesus, "Yes, Lord.

You know that I love You." Three times Peter denied Jesus around the smell of a charcoal fire, and three times Jesus commissioned him around the smell of a charcoal fire, telling him to tend or shepherd His sheep.[19] Because of this event, Peter could move forward. On the day of Pentecost, he preached with confidence in the mercy and grace of God. Jesus had redeemed the emotional pain of Peter's greatest mistake.

Jesus seeks to redeem our past painful events in the same way. After I left the Blacksburg, Virginia, area to go back to the church I had pastored before, I realized I had made a mistake in leaving, and it shamed me. But God sought to redeem the pain and my sense of failure. He sent me to Boone, North Carolina, for rest and healing, and once I was healed, He sent me back to the same place I had mistakenly left. I was able to participate with Him and others and plant Dwelling Place Christian Fellowship, where I still minister today. The place that was once a reminder of pain and failure is now the site of one of my greatest adventures in the Lord.

Isaiah 53:4 is a key passage for dealing with heartbreak. Not only did Jesus bear our sins, but He also bore the mental anguish of the death-filled events in our lives:

> *"Surely our griefs He Himself bore,*
> *And our sorrows He carried;*
> *Yet we ourselves esteemed Him stricken,*
> *Smitten of God, and afflicted."*

On the cross, Jesus spiritually carried the mental agony that this world of sin and death can produce in our souls. He bore the pain of the woman who was sexually abused. He bore the pain of a mother who lost a child. He bore the pain of war victims and the oppressed. Jesus cares about every facet of our being, and because of that, His work on the cross deals with every facet of sin and death. When I am ministering, I often pray Isaiah 53 over the person and then partner with the Holy Spirit as He heals that person's heart.

Negative soulish emotions from a past event can be altered in two ways:

1. The Lord ministers into them supernaturally during the course of life, or
2. We can partner with God through prayer and the ministry of His Word and Spirit to see healing in our emotions.

Whatever His method, the Lord wants to see our hearts healed and the emotions of past events altered to communicate His redeeming power.

The Lag Factor

When dealing with soulish emotions, we need to be aware of what I call the "lag factor." The lag factor is the gap in time between the revelation of truth and a change in our emotions.

Imagine a bear is chasing you through the woods. You manage to run into a house and slam the door — you are safe now. But when you first run inside, your emotions are in a very excited and fearful state. It will take a little bit of time for them to calm down to the point where they align with the truth of your safety. In that moment right after you shut the door, if you focus on what you are feeling, you will not be able to realize you are safe.

Soulish emotions can be generated quickly, but they lag as they come back in line with truth. It is not automatic. Our minds are not suddenly vacuum-sucked of fearful thoughts. There will be a lag in time before our emotions match our revelation of truth. If we're not careful, our negative emotions will cause us to start entertaining thoughts of fear again, which will cause our feelings of fear to escalate in intensity. In the midst of the lag factor, we need to hold fast to our revelation of truth and allow our emotions to catch up with that revelation. In the end, it comes down to doubt. Our doubt battles our conclusions of truth. The conclusions of the past wage war against the conclusions of the present, and that is what creates the lag factor.

I saw this process with a girl I will call Sarah. She was a senior at Virginia Tech, and for two or three years, she had been dating a guy I will call Kevin, who had graduated the year before. She was going to go see him during Thanksgiving break, and she was pretty excited that he might ask her to marry him.

The Sunday after Thanksgiving break, I saw her at the student center.

"Rick, can I talk to you?" she asked.

I thought, All right! Good. Kevin asked her to marry him.

But in my office, she sat down and burst into tears. She stumbled through the story. Kevin had broken up with her because he was in love with another girl. She was devastated. Then she said to me, "Rick, the Lord has really pressed into my heart, 'I know the plans I have for you.' I know that if Kevin comes back, it will be good — but I also know that if it's not Kevin, it will be good."

She held fast to the conclusion the Lord gave her. From Thanksgiving to spring, I watched as her pain lessened, but she didn't want to date anyone. One day, she told me, "John keeps asking me to coffee. But I just don't know if I want to go with anybody like that." She finally agreed to the coffee date, and to make a long story short, they got married and are in the ministry. A number of years ago, Sarah and John came to visit Paula and me, and their level of happiness was almost sickening. It was like one of Paula's chick flicks. Sarah knew what God had told her. She held fast to that revelation of truth, and gradually, her emotions came to line up with that truth.

Soulish emotions deal with conclusions. We run into the house to escape the bear. Our hearts are racing. We jump at every sound. But slowly, we begin to evaluate the situation and reach a conclusion: "I am safe." We then start to generate thoughts based on that conclusion: Okay, I'm safe. I don't have to feel afraid anymore. These thoughts will start to have an effect on us, and gradually, our hearts will calm and the emotions of fear will leave.

If someone comes along and touches me on the shoulder, I will feel it instantly. It is the same with spiritual emotions. If the Spirit of God touches us, the subsequent emotions are instantaneous. We immediately feel them. But with soulish emotions, there is a process of development that involves everything connected with those emotions: thoughts, feelings, beliefs, and actions.

When God speaks truth to us, we need to hold on to that truth and not let go, even if our emotions battle against it. Our hearts will calm. Our thoughts will sort themselves out. If we can hold on to the revelation of God's truth, we will eventually come to realize, Oh. I'm safe now.

Key Points of Chapter 8

When a virus infects a computer, the computer operator needs to run a virus scan. The virus scan identifies the location of the virus and then takes steps to remove it. In a similar way, our hearts can easily become infected with "viruses" of lies. It would be nice if we could run a virus scan every once in a while and remove all of those lies. Though we may not be able to do that exactly, we can allow our soulish emotions to reveal the "programming" in our hearts.

We know the process of soulish emotions:

1. An environment exposes a belief.
2. The belief generates thoughts.
3. The thoughts generate emotions.

With that in mind, we are able to work backward to see what is actually in our hearts. I use the phrase "tracking the emotion" to describe the process of using what I feel to reveal my heart's programming — that is, the conclusions it has stored. When we know what is in our hearts, we can partner with the Lord to bring change in our lives.

Responding to Soulish Emotions

The world often says, "If you feel something, you need to express it." But that can cause all sorts of problems. As believers, we want to take these steps whenever we feel something:

1. We identify whether or not the emotion is a soulish emotion.
2. We identify if it is positive or negative.
3. If it is negative, we respond in a way that brings healing and life.
4. If it is positive, we respond in a manner that accentuates the emotion and makes us more impressionable.

The Lord wants to see our hearts healed and the emotions of past events altered to communicate His redeeming power.

Notes / Reference Scriptures

1. Ephesians 4:26-27
2. 1 Peter 2:21-24
3. Matthew 23:25-26
4. 1 Timothy 6:9-10
5. Romans 8:4-6
6. Matthew 6:24-25; 1 John 2:15
7. John 12:31; 2 Corinthians 4:4
8. Ephesians 2:1-3
9. 1 Peter 2:11
10. Romans 6:12
11. Romans 6:1-7
12. Jeremiah 6:22-24
13. 1 Thessalonians 3:3-5
14. John 16:28-29
15. Mark 3:5; John 11:33-35
16. Ephesians 6:16
17. 2 Corinthians 10:3-5
18. John 18:18
19. John 21:15-17

PART FOUR

What Are Spiritual Emotions?

"Now we have received, not the spirit of the world, but the Spirit who is from God, so that we may know the things freely given to us by God, which things we also speak, not in words taught by human wisdom, but in those taught by the Spirit, combining spiritual thoughts with spiritual words.

"But a natural man does not accept the things of the Spirit of God, for they are foolishness to him; and he cannot understand them, because they are spiritually appraised. But he who is spiritual appraises all things, yet he himself is appraised by no one."

— 1 Corinthians 2:12–15

We live in a physical world, and understanding physical emotions is a very important part of living safely and healthily in this world.

We also live in the midst of a spiritual world. In the same way that physical emotions are important for living in the physical world, spiritual emotions are important for living in the spiritual world. God's desire is for us to understand all types of emotions—especially the spiritual.

Notice in 1 Corinthians 2:15 that the spiritual person appraises, or discerns, "all things." We want to be spiritual people who are able to discern what we are feeling physically, soulishly, and spiritually. This section of the book is written with the hope of empowering people into greater spiritual discernment.

The emotions of the human spirit are very different than the emotions of the body and soul. When we are born again, our spirits become one with the Holy Spirit,[18] so, naturally, there will be times when we feel what He is feeling. Feeling what the Holy Spirit feels is just one aspect of the emotions our spirits can sense.

9 An Introduction to Spiritual Emotions

When I was involved in campus ministry at Virginia Tech and Radford University, we had a situation that showed me the importance of spiritual emotions.

At the beginning of each new school year, a number of students would come to our meetings to check things out. One year, I sensed something in the spiritual realm that was particularly different. As the days and weeks passed, I was able to compare it to something I had sensed in the past when we were dealing with practicing witches and warlocks. The feeling gradually intensified. The spiritual atmosphere felt sticky and tainted with something I would just call nastiness. I called the student leadership together and told them I sensed a spirit of witchcraft at work in our ministry. We started praying that God's presence would reveal anything that was hidden in the dark. We also prayed that any curses spoken against us would return to the ones who sent them, so they would learn not to mess around with God's kids.

We discovered that one of the new students who had started attending our meetings was a practicing witch. She was taking pictures of people in our ministry and shipping them back home to her coven, which was using the pictures as a focal point to cast curses on our ministry. When we discovered this, we prayed for her and reached out to her even more with the love of Jesus.

The spiritual pressure became so great that the new student withdrew from school and moved back to her hometown. But as she was moving out, some of our students helped her pack, and she ended up praying to receive Jesus as her Lord and Savior. That student experienced the salvation of God because of spiritual emotions — we had sensed what was going on in the spiritual realm.

Remember that every emotion is a signal of an event — something is happening in us or around us. The emotions in the spirit are unique and different from those in the flesh and soul. In this section of the book, we will discuss the reality of spiritual emotions and then seek to understand what to do with them.

The following statement is our working definition of spiritual emotions:

> *A spiritual emotion is a signal of an event that has occurred, is occurring, or will occur in a person or in that person's spiritual environment, the spiritual realm, or the physical realm.*

When we break down that definition a bit more, we discover some interesting things:

1. Spiritual emotions exist.
2. Spiritual emotions are timeless; they are not confined to the here and now.
3. Spiritual emotions can mean sensing the signals of past, present, or future events.
4. The truths signaled by the spiritual emotion can be from an event that is occurring inside of us (something happening within us) or around us (in the spiritual realm or corresponding physical realm).

I can be in an awesome worship service and feel love, joy, and peace. I can be in that same type of worship service later on and feel distant, far-off, and like part of me wants to run away, even though everyone around me is having a great time in the Lord. What is it I am feeling? In both of these situations, spiritual emotions could very well be at work.

Spiritual emotions are a distinct reality with every one of us, as well as in the Word of God. It is very important for us to discern what is being spiritually signaled and then take appropriate action.

Emotions of Our Spirits

In Luke 1:47, Mary, pregnant with Jesus, was greeted by her cousin Elizabeth, who was pregnant with John the Baptist. Mary declared, "My spirit has rejoiced in God my Savior." Her spirit felt joy at meeting with her cousin. That is a spiritual emotion. Her spirit was signaling the reality of a current spiritual event.

Paula and I know many people who are important in our lives. Two of those people are Mitch and Leigha Semones, who have been involved with us in ministry for more than twenty years. They know just about everything there is to know about us. Leigha is very sensitive to the spiritual realm. I kid around with her that while most of our spirits are like the small satellite dishes used at residences, she is like one of those giant satellite dishes used to listen to radio signals from outer space. She picks up on everything that is "broadcasted" into the spiritual realm.

For many years, she assumed she was feeling only her own emotions, and consequently, she sank into depression, rejection, fear, isolation, and sorrow. Mitch would try to comfort her without fully knowing what was going on. However, as the Lord taught us about the reality of spiritual emotions, Leigha discovered that most of the things she feels come from the people around her. These emotions are not "her."

She will often call me and tell me what she is feeling, and her feelings match the things going on in the church or what I am dealing with in ministry. If Paula and I are struggling with discouragement, she frequently feels it. She has trouble sitting in the back of the room during worship services because she becomes distracted with all of the soulish and spiritual pain in the lives of the people in the congregation.

I have ministered to a significant number of people like Leigha who can sense things in the spiritual realm, but they do not know or understand what they are feeling. It is important for us to understand how spiritual emotions work and how God created us to feel them. If we do not understand how He made us to function in the spiritual realm, we can experience many frustrations and pains He did not purpose for us to experience. A lack of knowledge in these things can produce difficult consequences.

The Variety of Spiritual Emotions

Every person can experience a wide range of spiritual emotions. On one end of the spectrum, spiritual emotions can communicate joy, as in Luke 1:47. On the other end of the spectrum, a person can spiritually experience grief or sorrow, as when Jesus went to comfort Mary and Martha and to raise Lazarus from the dead.[1] It was Jesus' spirit that was grieved. Years later when Paul entered the city of Athens, he experienced a provoking, or discomfort, in his spirit: *"Now while Paul was waiting for them at Athens, his spirit was being provoked within him as he was observing the city full of idols"* (Acts 17:16). Paul's spirit felt the unrighteousness of the city. His distress was caused by the effects of the sin permeating Athens.

Remember that God is Spirit, and when we are born again, our spirits become one with His Spirit. This means that there will be times when we feel what He is feeling. On several occasions in my life, His spiritual presence has become so real to

me that I end up laughing with joy. He feels joy, so I feel joy
in His presence:

> *"You will make known to me the path of life;*
> *In Your presence is fullness of joy;*
> *In Your right hand there are pleasures forever."*
> — Psalm 16:11

> *"When the Lord brought back the captive ones of Zion,*
> *We were like those who dream.*
> *Then our mouth was filled with laughter*
> *And our tongue with joyful shouting;*
> *Then they said among the nations,*
> *'The Lord has done great things for them.'*
> *Those who sow in tears shall reap with joyful shouting."*
> — Psalm 126:1-2, 5

However, I have also experienced times with God when
all I could do was cry with sorrow as He expressed to me His
heart for His children who were suffering. One day, a small
group of women and I were ministering to a young woman
who had suffered a lot of pain in her relationship with her
family. God began to pour His emotions for her into my heart.
The pain became so strong within me that all I could do was
sob as I tried to communicate His heart for her.

When the apostle John was "in the spirit" on the Lord's
day and Jesus appeared to him, all he could do was fall on
his face in reverence. The awesomeness of God overwhelmed
him. Whenever this has happened to me, it has happened
in worship. God's holy presence would become so great, so
strong, that I would not want to move or even breathe.

Spiritual emotions cannot be put in a box. They are varied
in their actual feelings and expressions.

Spiritually Discerning

An awesome woman of God, Minnie Coleman, came to our church a number of years ago to minister to our body. Without knowing anything that was going on in the church, she warned us about a particular demonic spirit that was attacking us. At first, I did not totally understand her warning, but as I researched that particular spirit's characteristics in God's Word, I realized she was right. Her spiritual discernment helped us gain victory over something that had numbed us to its presence. We had lost our spiritual discernment in that particular area and did not see what was going on.

One crucial aspect of operating in spiritual discernment is being able to understand spiritual emotions. Jesus tells us in John 3:8 that life in the Spirit is like following the wind. We cannot see the wind to follow it, but we can feel the wind; we can see its effects, and we can hear it. We need to learn to hear the voice of the Holy Spirit and be able to discern His effects. We also need to learn how to discern the spiritual realm in and around us. That is why the Book of Hebrews declares that the mature person has his or her "senses trained" to discern good from evil.[2] In the next few paragraphs, I am going to suggest some ways we can develop spiritual discernment.

Knowing the Difference

We are soulish beings[3] living in a physical body, having been born into a physical world. The human spirit has a need to communicate with its Maker. That Maker, a spiritual Being, lives and exists in the spiritual realm, which is more real and eternal than the physical realm.[4] We learn how to live and survive in the physical world by understanding its components and movements—but we have a need to relate to our spiritual God and function in His spiritual realm. Whether we know it or not, both realms interact together all of the time, and our survival often depends on our ability to understand the interaction between those two realms.

> *"For though we walk in the flesh, we do not war according to the flesh, for the weapons of our warfare are not of the flesh, but divinely powerful for the destruction of fortresses. We are destroying speculations and every lofty thing raised up against the knowledge of God, and we are taking every thought captive to the obedience of Christ."*
> — 2 Corinthians 10:3-5

> *"For our struggle is not against flesh and blood, but against the rulers, against the powers, against the world forces of this darkness, against the spiritual forces of wickedness in the heavenly places."* — Ephesians 6:12

As soulish beings, learning to understand and walk in both the physical realm and the spiritual realm can be a challenge. We can easily come to depend solely on our intellect. Since the fleshly world can be overwhelming, it is also easy to become fleshly in our thinking, therefore losing our capacity to understand the depths of God's Word and His heart for us. Because the spiritual realm is invisible, sometimes it can be very difficult to submit to God's existence in that realm, but we cannot survive apart from our heavenly Father — our souls have a deep need to walk and communicate in the spiritual realm with God. Balancing the physical, soulish, and spiritual is an important aspect of living a healthy life.

Paul addresses this need in 1 Corinthians. In chapter 3, he shows the distinction between fleshly and spiritual Christians:

> *"And I, brethren, could not speak to you as to spiritual men, but as to men of flesh, as to infants in Christ. I gave you milk to drink, not solid food; for you were not yet able to receive it. Indeed, even now you are not yet able, for you are still fleshly. For since there is jealousy and strife among you, are you not fleshly, and are you not walking like mere men?"* — 1 Corinthians 3:1-3

God's will for us is to live as spiritual men and women who are able to discern what is going on and how we should respond in the physical and spiritual realms. Paul could not speak to the Corinthian church as if they were spiritual men and women because they were fleshly (worldly or physical) in their thinking. The external appearance of the Corinthian church suggested they were a spiritually oriented church, but Paul knew they were fleshly. They did not have spiritual discernment. As a result of being fleshly in their thinking, they were not able to handle the things of the Spirit.

The description of the soulish Christian can be found in 1 Corinthians 2:14–15:

> *"But a natural [literally 'soulish'] man does not accept the things of the Spirit of God, for they are foolishness to him; and he cannot understand them, because they are spiritually appraised. But he who is spiritual appraises all things, yet he himself is appraised by no one."*

Paul writes in this passage that the natural or soulish man cannot discern the things of the spiritual realm, but the spiritual man can discern or appraise "all things": those of the spiritual realm and of the world. So we see in these passages that neither the soulish person nor the fleshly person can have spiritual discernment and wisdom.

Understanding the Movements of the Spiritual Realm

We need spiritual wisdom if we are going to discern and walk effectively as men and women of God in the spiritual realm. It is for this reason that Paul prayed for spiritual wisdom:

> *"For this reason also, since the day we heard of it, we have not ceased to pray for you and to ask that you may be filled with the knowledge of His will in all spiritual wisdom and understanding, so that you will walk in a manner worthy of the Lord."* — Colossians 1:9–10

Wisdom is the understanding of movements. When we say that a person has worldly wisdom, we mean that the person knows and understands how the elements of the world move and interact. Spiritual wisdom understands the movements of the spiritual realm, especially the movements of God's Spirit. So when a person has spiritual wisdom, that person understands and discerns what is occurring in the spiritual realm.

Testing the Spirits

"Beloved, do not believe every spirit, but test the spirits to see whether they are from God, because many false prophets have gone out into the world." — 1 John 4:1

With the wisdom and discernment the Lord gives us, we are to test or prove the spirits that come across our path. John writes that we shouldn't believe or accept something simply because it is supernatural or at first appears to be a positive experience. In 1 John 4:1, John is addressing the problem of false prophets (people who are speaking out of pain or agenda). He says to test the speaker's spirit. One way we test a person's spirit is by comparing his or her words with the Word of God, as the Berean Christians did in Acts 17:11. They tested the things they heard by comparing them with the Scriptures. Obviously, everything a prophet proclaims has to be in line with the written Word of God. God will never contradict Himself. He will never speak something that does not line up with His written Word or His character.

Spiritual emotions are one of the most important tools we can use to test the spirit of what we are hearing. In Matthew 7:15–16, Jesus reveals the foundation for testing spirits:

"Beware of the false prophets, who come to you in sheep's clothing, but inwardly are ravenous wolves. You will know them by their fruits. Grapes are not gathered from thorn bushes nor figs from thistles, are they?"

If we want to test someone or something, we look at the fruit. There are at least two kinds of fruit—the fruit of relationship and the fruit of ministry[5]—but later in Matthew 7, Jesus says that the fruit of ministry (prophecy, healing, and deliverance) does not validate a person's relationship with the Lord. Knowing God is the only thing that matters. Knowing Him is the fruit of relationship. It is possible for the fruit of ministry to be quite overwhelming and deceiving at times.

The fruit of relationship with God is the fruit of the Spirit. It verifies relationship with Him: *"But the fruit of the Spirit is love, joy, peace, patience, kindness, goodness, faithfulness, gentleness, self-control; against such things there is no law"* (Galatians 5:22–23). Many people who are operating out of pain or who have an agenda start off saying things that sound right doctrinally. We won't always be able to hear someone speak and automatically know if he or she supports God's purposes and heart. Therefore, the key to testing someone's spirit is sensing that person's relationship to the fruit of the Spirit. Our spirits feel what is happening in the spiritual realm as that person speaks:

> *"Speaking the truth in love, we are to grow up in all aspects into Him who is the head, even Christ."*
> — Ephesians 4:15

> *"Who among you is wise and understanding? Let him show by his good behavior his deeds in the gentleness of wisdom. But if you have bitter jealousy and selfish ambition in your heart, do not be arrogant and so lie against the truth. This wisdom is not that which comes down from above, but is earthly, natural, demonic. For where jealousy and selfish ambition exist, there is disorder and every evil thing. But the wisdom from above is first pure, then peaceable, gentle, reasonable, full of mercy and good fruits, unwavering, without hypocrisy. And the seed whose fruit is righteousness is sown in peace by those who make peace."*
> — James 3:13–18

We use the emotions of the Spirit's fruit to test the spirits of the prophets and teachers we encounter. I have heard a number of preachers and leaders say things that were doctrinally sound, but as I listened with my spirit as well as my ears, I realized that something was "off." The fruit of the Spirit was absent in their words, and as time passed, their actions behind the scenes became visible and did not align with God's truth. We will talk more about discerning spirits later in this book, but for now, all of us need to train ourselves to know the fruit of relationship with God as it corresponds to spiritual emotions. We then can use that "fruit" to test the spirits we encounter.

Discerning with Grace

Walking in the realm of discernment can be tricky, especially when we pick up on something negative in another person. In the early days, I would get around people and start feeling things that were harmful, and I incorrectly assumed these emotions were my own. I thought, I have issues! But I began realizing that I was feeling what was going on in the person near me. This isn't my issue. I'm sensing a stronghold or a spirit harassing this other person.

We can sense another person's struggle with anger, greed, lust, fear, anxiety—the list goes on. How do we begin to discern if it is someone else's emotion and not our own? First, we check to see if we are dealing with a physical emotion. Is this emotion originating somewhere in our bodies? If it isn't, we move on to the realm of the soul: Do we feel this way because of the direction of our thoughts? If it isn't a physical or soulish emotion, then we are discerning something spiritual.

Whenever we sense something is amiss in another person, we have to remember that we can judge the action, but we don't judge the person.[6] If someone tells me a lie, I can judge that action. I can say, "Joe, that's a lie. That's not who you are. Speak truth."[7] But I would be judging that person if I responded, "You told me a lie, and that makes you a liar!" That would be pronouncing sentence on who that person is.

We are not to judge our neighbors. James 4:12 asks, *"There is only one Lawgiver and Judge, the One who is able to save and to destroy; but who are you who judge your neighbor?"* We have no right to pronounce a sentence on someone's life, but we can use our emotions to recognize what is going on in the people around us and then speak life and wholeness into them.

The Function of the Human Spirit

In the beginning of this chapter, I defined spiritual emotions as signals of events within us or around us. Our spirits can signal many different kinds of events. In order to fully understand spiritual emotions, we first need to lay a foundation for understanding the function of the human spirit.

Every person born into this world has a spirit. When God created our forefather Adam, He *"breathed into his nostrils the breath of life [spirit]; and man became a living being [soul]"* (Genesis 2:7). The human spirit has three main functions.

Life to the Body

> *"For just as the body without the spirit is dead, so also faith without works is dead."* — James 2:26

The first function of the human spirit is to give life to the body. Solomon describes the human spirit as the "silver cord" that connects the soul to the body:

> *"For man goes to his eternal home while mourners go about in the street. Remember Him before **the silver cord is broken** and the golden bowl is crushed, the pitcher by the well is shattered and the wheel at the cistern is*

> *crushed; then the dust will return to the earth as it was, and the spirit will return to God who gave it."*
> — Ecclesiastes 12:5–7, (emphasis added)

I was in the hospital room when my mother died. Before death, she was weak and sick, but when she died, her soul and spirit departed from her body. Even though it was painful for me, I saw a noticeable transformation occur. That transformation at the point of death was spiritual in nature; the spirit and soul left to be with Jesus.

Communication Link

The second function of the human spirit is that it is our communication link with the spiritual realm.

I picture the human spirit like Wi-Fi capability on a computer. Wi-Fi capability allows us to connect with the Internet and communicate with the rest of the world. The computer would be isolated if it did not have this capability. In the same way, if we did not have a spirit, we would be isolated and unable to communicate with the spiritual realm around us; it would be like the control tower at an airport trying to direct a pilot without a radio. In order to communicate with each other, both parties need a radio. If we are going to talk with God and follow His leading, we have to have a spirit, which enables us to hear and respond to His promptings.

Our heavenly Father's desire is for us to know Him.[8] He is a spiritual Being, and when we come to Him, we must come to Him in spirit and truth.[9] The main reason God created us with this ability to communicate with the spiritual realm was so we could have an intimate relationship with Him.

When we are born again, our spirits are made new and connected to the Holy Spirit. At that time, God seeks to communicate to us His passion for our identity as His sons and daughters. He speaks to us in a spiritual language and frequency:

"Now we have received, not the spirit of the world, but the Spirit who is from God, so that we may know the things freely given to us by God, which things we also speak, not in words taught by human wisdom, but in those taught by the Spirit, combining spiritual thoughts with spiritual words."   — 1 Corinthians 2:12–13

The Holy Spirit Himself bears witness with our spirits that we are children of God.[10]

The human spirit is a communication, or sensory, link with the spiritual realm as a whole. In addition to sensing and communicating with God, we can also sense the presence of angels and demons, which we will talk about in the next chapter.

Interacts with the Human Heart

The third function of the spirit is the way it interacts with the "inner man" or heart.[11] Remember that the heart contains the programming, or conclusions, of our lives. Those conclusions determine everything we see, hear, speak, feel, believe, do, and love. Therefore, our spirits' interaction with our hearts is vital for our existence with God.

The spirit interacts with the heart in three ways, and each one is very significant when we are seeking freedom for ourselves or ministering freedom to another person:

1. The spirit reveals the heart's programming,
2. The heart determines the information the spirit sends to God, and
3. The heart processes the information the spirit receives from God.

Let's look at each of these ways more closely.

The Programming of the Heart

"The spirit of man is the lamp of the Lord,
Searching all the innermost parts of his being."
— Proverbs 20:27

When a traumatic event occurs in a person's life, that event can be pushed down and locked in the depths of the heart. As a result of the trauma, symptoms like fear, anxiety, or depression can arise. Some counselors use drugs or techniques like hypnosis in an effort to unlock the pain, but the Lord gave each person a spirit to reveal and search these problem areas.

Proverbs 20:27 states that the Lord created our spirits to search out and reveal the depths of our hearts. I see a person's spirit like a flashlight-toting detective who is investigating a large house with many rooms. The spirit silently examines and reveals the contents of every room in that house. When I am ministering to people, I often pray Proverbs 20:27 over them, and they frequently end up remembering events of sin or pain they have not thought about in years. As the events are brought into the light, they can be dealt with appropriately and healed.

Communication with God

"[I pray that] the God of our Lord Jesus Christ, the Father of glory, may give to you a spirit of wisdom and of revelation in the knowledge of Him. I pray that the eyes of your heart may be enlightened, so that you will know what is the hope of His calling, what are the riches of the glory of His inheritance in the saints."
— Ephesians 1:17–18

In the original Greek, this passage is grammatically structured to communicate that the heart is enlightened so that the spirit may function in wisdom and knowledge. In other words, how we function and operate in the spirit comes out of the programming of our hearts. If our hearts are enlightened with the knowledge of God, our spirits will have wisdom and revelation. As an example of this, when we pray in tongues, our spirits are praying. However, if there is a stronghold (something that blocks us off from God's presence, provisions, or truth) in our hearts about the legitimacy of spiritual gifts, our spirits will be shut down in that area, and we will be hindered in praying in the spirit.

A woman in our church was miraculously baptized in the Holy Spirit at a retreat. When she came home, you could see the difference in her countenance and confidence. I asked her if she had prayed in tongues when the event occurred, and she said she hadn't. As I prayed about it, I saw her holding a gift, but it was encased in a shell and unable to function. She later had a vision of a mental stronghold that was crippling her in the things of the spirit. After she dealt with the stronghold, I prayed a simple prayer like, "Lord, I loosen my sister's spirit to function in Jesus' name." Immediately, she began to pray in the spirit beautifully and freely. The traditions of religion[12] planted in her heart were crippling her spirit from functioning as God had purposed it to function.

Faith is one of the most powerful forces in the spiritual realm — it is a spiritual principle. If we are going to come to God, we must believe in Him. Romans 10:10 tells us, *"With the heart a person believes."* Doubt, the antithesis of faith and believing, also occurs in the heart.[13] So if our hearts are filled with doubt, our spirits will not be effective in touching and reaching the heart of God.[14] Paul gives additional revelation concerning this truth in 1 Corinthians 2:9–11:

> *"But just as it is written,*
> *'Things which eye has not seen and ear has not heard,*
> *And which have not entered the heart of man,*
> *All that God has prepared for those who love Him.'*
> *For to us God revealed them through the Spirit; for the*
> *Spirit searches all things, even the depths of God. For*
> *who among men knows the thoughts [depths] of a man*

except the spirit of the man which is in him? Even so the thoughts [depths] of God no one knows except the Spirit of God."

The Holy Spirit reveals what is in the depths of God. The Holy Spirit is perfectly submitted to the Father, and He reveals only truth, which comes from the Father through Jesus Christ:

"But when He, the Spirit of truth, comes, He will guide you into all the truth; for He will not speak on His own initiative, but whatever He hears, He will speak; and He will disclose to you what is to come. He will glorify Me, for He will take of Mine and will disclose it to you. All things that the Father has are Mine; therefore I said that He takes of Mine and will disclose it to you."
— John 16:13–15

When the Holy Spirit speaks, He reveals what He hears, or is given, and His revelation of God comes out of the depths of God. This is the same spiritual process that works in humanity. What the human spirit reveals and releases comes out of the depths of that person. So when we communicate with God, we communicate with Him from the depths of our hearts through our spirits. That is why we see God putting so much emphasis on the heart of a man or woman throughout Scripture. The person who speaks truth in his or her heart is the one who may dwell in His presence:

"O Lord, who may abide in Your tent?
Who may dwell on Your holy hill?
He who walks with integrity, and works righteousness,
And speaks truth in his heart."
— Psalm 15:1–2

It is our hearts, not our conscious minds, that tell our spirits what to say to God and what to do with Him.

Processor of Information

"Blessed are the pure in heart, for they shall see God."
— Matthew 5:8

If we come to God, it will be in, or by, the spirit. The heart is that part of us that enables us to see God in the spirit, so if our hearts are not pure, we won't be able to see Him, because He is pure and holy.[15]

Revisiting an analogy I used earlier, the relationship between our hearts and our spirits can be compared to the relationship between a computer's Wi-Fi capability and its program-containing hard drive. If a computer receives a file formatted for one type of program but the hard drive does not have the ability to read that type of file, the computer won't be able to process the information. God could be pouring His truth into us, but we are unable to "access" that truth because our hearts are not open to it; they are not correctly "programmed."

Earlier in this book, I shared the testimony of a young woman who had been sexually abused by her dad. Pain filled her soul. She had been crying out to God for His comfort but had not experienced it, which angered her toward Him. One reason abuse and rape are so traumatic is that Satan seeks to twist and distort the situation so the woman ends up believing it was her fault. The female heart can easily receive the lie that she could have done something to prevent the rape or abuse — that it was her fault. Once this false conclusion of condemnation is established, the woman often begins to feel and believe that her heavenly Father has abandoned her in the midst of her pain.

As I ministered to the young woman that night, the Lord started speaking to me about how we are made and that we can dictate how we receive from the Lord in the spirit. The Lord is very tender toward us and He will not usurp our will, especially not the will of a person who has been taken advantage of. He will not force our will or our ability to choose. If

He did, how would He be any different than those who abuse others?

After a woman has been abused, the enemy's goal is to con her into condemning herself. While I ministered to this woman, the Lord reminded me of 1 John 3:21: *"Beloved, if our heart does not condemn us, we have confidence before God."* Her heart condemned her. It dictated what she could and could not receive from God and did not enable her to have confidence before Him. Remember that confidence is the crucial attribute that enables us to come into God's presence.

The place she needed to go in the spirit was the Throne of Grace, where she could receive mercy and find grace to help and comfort her in her time of need.[16] However, her heart had been "programmed" with self-condemnation, and that programming was stealing her confidence, not allowing her to receive the comfort she needed. Her heavenly Father was reaching out to her, but her heart was not allowing her to receive from Him.

I led this precious woman in asking God to forgive her for entertaining the lie that this event had been her fault. She also confessed the truth concerning the matter: She was not the initiator of the abuse. The daughter does not have the responsibility of taking care of the dad, but the dad has the responsibility of taking care of the daughter. She immediately started weeping, releasing the pain that was stored down in her heart.

I have witnessed similar scenarios hundreds of times. The enemy causes a woman's heart to be shut down with condemnation, which steals her confidence to come into her Father's loving presence. In most of these situations, the woman entertains thoughts like, I am not good enough for God, or, I am dirty; therefore, I cannot come to Him. This type of thought pattern typically generates feelings of loneliness, pain, depression, and fear. I have actually had women in these situations tell me that God had left them and was not coming to them. But that was not true. God had not turned from them — their condemning hearts literally cut off their spirits from His love and comfort.

If people endured abusive childhoods and their conclusion about being a child is painful, their hearts will not receive any information from their spirits regarding their identity as children of God. They don't want that truth. For them, being a child means to be in pain. So the Spirit is saying, "Child," and the people are frantically resisting. I don't want that! I don't want to be a child!

If a woman has been abused by her dad or other male relatives, the pain in her heart will most likely make it hard for her to trust men, and she will be tempted to control males in her adult life, including God the Father. She could find it difficult to develop an intimate spiritual relationship with Him because of the fear of pain stored in her heart. All of this has to do with the heart's programming. The antidote is to release the lies and be healed of the pain. Once our hearts are healed, our spirits are free to bask in our Father's goodness.

Our hearts process the information that our spirits receive from God, so we continually need to examine and guard our hearts.

It is exciting and humbling to consider that an all-powerful, all-knowing God would care to communicate with human beings. So we could intimately interact with Him, God created each of us with a spirit, which opened up all kinds of possibilities for us—things that even angels long to look into.[17] The entire spiritual realm became open to us through our spirits. The most important spiritual interaction a person could have is that between his or her spirit and the Holy Spirit.

Key Points of Chapter 9

Spiritual emotions signal an event in the spiritual realm that affects our spirits. That event can be internal (something within us) or external (something within our spiritual environment). Unlike physical and soulish emotions, the emotions of the spirit are not constrained to events of the past and present. With our spirits, we can also sense and feel future events. This occurs because our spirits are united with God's Spirit, who knows all things.

The Function of the Human Spirit

1. The human spirit gives life to the body.
2. The human spirit is the communication link with the spiritual realm.
3. The human spirit interacts with the depths of the human heart.

How the Human Spirit Interacts with the Heart

1. The spirit reveals the heart's programming.
2. The heart determines the information the spirit sends to God.
3. The heart processes the information the spirit receives from God.

Notes / Reference Scriptures

1. John 11:33-35
2. Hebrews 5:14
3. 1 Corinthians 15:45-49
4. 2 Corinthians 4:16-18
5. Romans 1:13
6. Matthew 7:1-6
7. Colossians 3:9
8. John 17:3
9. John 4:13-24
10. Romans 8:16
11. 1 Corinthians 2:11
12. Mark 7:8-13
13. Mark 11:23
14. James 1:5-7
15. Titus 1:15
16. Hebrews 4:16
17. 1 Peter 1
18. 1 Corinthians 6:17

Coloring Outside the Lines:
How External Events Can Cause Spiritual Emotions

A few years ago, I went to a new hair salon. No one was behind the reception desk, but the beauticians in the back told me to go ahead and sign in.

As I was signing my name on their log, one of the beauticians came running up to me. She told me it wasn't her turn to take a client, but she was going to go ahead and cut my hair anyway. She was very friendly with me, and right away, I began to sense a spirit of adultery on her. I cannot tolerate this, I thought. I have to do something. I asked the Lord for a prophetic word for her.

She told me she was a single mom who had recently gone through a divorce. As she cut my hair, the Lord answered my request and flooded my mind with words for her. I told her what God was sharing with me, and she started to cry. The more I spoke to her, the harder she cried and the faster she cut my hair. At one point, she had to excuse herself so she could go into the back room and blow her nose. We continued our conversation when she returned, and she ended up cutting my hair far shorter than I wanted.

When I got home, Paula's first words to me were, "Who cut your hair?!"

I was sensing the beautician's spiritual environment with my spirit. When I sensed it, I had to make some choices. It is one thing to sense something in the spiritual realm, and it is quite another thing to know exactly what you are sensing and then respond appropriately. This chapter will give some insight into the external events our spirits can sense.

In the last chapter, we looked at the function of the human spirit. It gives life to our physical bodies, acting as the tether that holds our souls to our bodies. Our spirits also interact with our hearts and minds and serve as our communication link with the spiritual realm. In the same way we use our physical bodies to touch the physical realm, we use our spirits to reach into the spiritual realm. What can we feel externally in the spiritual realm? The simple answer is anything. Our spirits can even "pick up" on an external event somewhere else in the world. Keep in mind that the timing of these events can fluctuate — they could have already occurred, or they are occurring or will occur.

I am grateful to my friend Radovan Bogdanovic, who pointed out to me that the spirit receives information — that is, it senses emotions — from a number of different external sources. As I researched the subject, I found there are at least four external sources from which our spirits can sense emotions:

1. God,
2. The spiritual realm (we can feel the presence of demonic or angelic influences),
3. A spiritual environment, and
4. Other people.

Feeling and Sensing God

"Now we have received, not the spirit of the world, but the Spirit who is from God, so that we may know the things freely given to us by God." — 1 Corinthians 2:12

I was spending some quality "Jesus time" with a prophet who has the ability to see in the spirit. As we were talking about the Lord and His amazingness, I began to feel a sweet and wonderful presence in the room.

The prophet suddenly said, "There He is!"

"Who?" I asked.

"Jesus," he quickly answered.

I was awed at the awesomeness of the Lord in that moment. I had not shared what I was feeling with anyone, but someone else—in an entirely different manner—verified the emotion I was sensing.

God created us to have relationship with Him, to be able to communicate with Him, and to interact with the spiritual realm. In Ephesians 2:22, Paul talks about the opportunity we have to interact with God, *"in whom you also are being built together into a dwelling of God in the Spirit."* God dwells in us, and He desires to walk with us. He reveals Himself to us in the spirit. We communicate with Him and know Him through His Word, hearing His voice, and seeing His effects as He moves and works in and around us. We can also communicate with Him through the emotions of our spirits.

If I interact with Paula, I can physically feel her. The closer I get to her, the more I can physically feel her. In a similar way, God lives and exists in the spiritual realm. He is a spiritual Being, and when we interact with Him, we can spiritually sense, or feel, His presence. The further we venture into His presence, the more intensely we can feel Him. When John had a close encounter with the resurrected Jesus in Revelation 1, he was overcome by Jesus' presence. He fell at His feet like a dead man. When Isaiah saw the unveiled holiness of God, he was overcome by its reality and repented of his sin (Isaiah 6).

What does God feel like? Simply put, God feels like joy, peace, and love.

God's Presence and Joy

David tells us there is fullness of joy when we are in God's presence:

> *"You will make known to me the path of life;*
> *In Your presence is fullness of joy;*
> *In Your right hand there are pleasures forever."*
> — Psalm 16:11

> *"For You make him most blessed forever;*
> *You make him joyful with gladness in Your presence."*
> — Psalm 21:6

Based on these verses and others, I would suggest that we cannot be in God's presence without feeling and sensing His joy, for He is the God of joy. As I mentioned in an earlier chapter, joy is not the same emotion as happiness. Happiness is an emotion that is based on good "happenings." If our happenings are bad, we will be un-happy.

Joy, on the other hand, is a spiritual emotion that is an expression of God's character. One of my favorite passages in Scripture is 1 Timothy 6:17, which ends with this line: *"God, who richly supplies us with all things to enjoy."* The nature of our God is joy, and subsequently, He delights in giving us things to enjoy.

Even the major provision of God's grace has joy in its very fabric. The root of the Greek word meaning "grace" (charis) is joy (chara). Therefore, the grace of God is literally the expression of His joy.

Several times, the fullness of God's presence has inspired me and released joy into my soul, and there was so much joy that I could not contain the laughter that filled me.[1] Every time this has happened to me, I am amazed at the greatness and the preciousness of the Spirit of God.

God's Presence and Peace

Peace is another emotion we will feel when we are in God's presence. God revealed His nature and character in the Old Testament through His names, and one of the Old Testament names for God is Jehovah-Shalom, which means *"The God [or Lord] of Peace."* Judges 6:24 takes it one step further by saying, "Gideon built an altar there to the Lord and named it The Lord is Peace." Peace is God's nature and character. He does not simply contain peace — He is peace.

God is called the God of Peace in the New Testament as well,[2] and Jesus tells us that in Him, we have peace. Peace is the dividing point between Jesus and the world:

> *"These things I have spoken to you, so that in Me you may have peace. In the world you have tribulation, but take courage; I have overcome the world."*
>
> — John 16:33

If anything in us is attached to the world, the result is tribulation. But everything in us that is attached to Jesus knows peace. So we can confidently say that one of the emotions of God's presence is peace.

God's Presence and Love

All that being said, however, the preeminent emotion of God is love:

> *"Beloved, let us love one another, for love is from God; and everyone who loves is born of God and knows God. The one who does not love does not know God, for God is love."*
>
> — 1 John 4:7–8

As it is with peace, God does not simply possess love—He is love. His very nature is love. In fact, according to 1 John 4:7-8, love is one of the main indicators God has given us to tell us whether or not we know Him. We cannot be around God and not sense His love: *"Righteousness and justice are the foundation of Your throne; lovingkindness and truth go before You"* (Psalm 89:14). This passage tells me that when we approach God, the first thing we will sense is His lovingkindness.

To be in God's presence is to feel His love, and that love will naturally spread through our lives and be expressed through us to others. If we want to increase our revelation of God, we simply need to open our hearts to love Him in a greater measure. With the increase of love comes an increase in our revelation of Him:

> *"Knowledge makes arrogant, but love edifies. If anyone supposes that he knows anything, he has not yet known as he ought to know; but if anyone loves God, he is known by Him."* — 1 Corinthians 8:1-3

There are many other emotions we can feel when we are in God's unhindered presence. He promises us that when we come to know Him as our Lord and Savior, the Holy Spirit will dwell in us.[3] God also promises He will walk and move among us. His presence can be awesome, holy, powerful, and majestic. Personally, when I experience His manifold presence, my senses are overloaded. My "fuses" are blown. I feel His absolute power, while also feeling the intense comfort of His love. The fullness of joy fills my soul, but at the same time, He is so incredible and holy that I do not want to move out of reverence for Him.

Sensing Spiritual Beings

As we discussed, the human spirit is a communication link with the spiritual realm. That realm contains more than God alone. Not only can we sense God's presence, but through our spirits we can also sense the presence of spiritual beings, both angels and demons.

We see this in Daniel 10:5-7 when he had a visitation from an angel of the Lord. Notice what happened to the men who were with Daniel:

> "I lifted my eyes and looked, and behold, there was a certain man dressed in linen, whose waist was girded with a belt of pure gold of Uphaz. His body also was like beryl, his face had the appearance of lightning, his eyes were like flaming torches, his arms and feet like the gleam of polished bronze, and the sound of his words like the sound of a tumult. Now I, Daniel, alone saw the vision, while the men who were with me did not see the vision; nevertheless, a great dread fell on them, and they ran away to hide themselves."

When the angel manifested himself to Daniel, his companions could not physically see the angel — but they certainly could feel his presence. Their souls and intellects did not help them in this case; they discerned, or felt, the angel spiritually. Their spiritual discernment was so great that the men ran and hid themselves in fear.

In the Book of Job, Eliphaz, one of Job's friends, told of an experience in which a spirit appeared to him:

> "Now a word was brought to me stealthily,
> And my ear received a whisper of it.
> Amid disquieting thoughts from the visions of the night,
> When deep sleep falls on men,
> Dread came upon me, and trembling,
> And made all my bones shake.
> "Then a spirit passed by my face;
> The hair of my flesh bristled up.

It stood still, but I could not discern its appearance;
A form was before my eyes;
There was silence, then I heard a voice:
'Can mankind be just before God?
Can a man be pure before his Maker?'" — Job 4:12–17

Notice how he could sense the spirit's presence before anything was seen or said. Many of us know the feeling that Eliphaz described. I have experienced times when a sudden cold chill hit me, and I knew something evil was around. At other times, I have sensed something powerful and angelic around me. Daniel 10:5–7 and Job 4:12–17 are good examples of a person's spirit being able to sense the presence of spiritual beings, whether they are from God or from the devil.

Sensing Spiritual Environments

"Now while Paul was waiting for them at Athens, his spirit was being provoked within him as he was observing the city full of idols." — Acts 17:16

Our spiritual emotions can also signal a spiritual environment—the spiritual atmosphere of our current location or the place we are thinking or praying about. Acts 17:16 shows us the spiritual environment of the city of Athens. That environment was not caused by the idols themselves, for Paul writes in 1 Corinthians 10:19–21 that an idol, in and of itself, is nothing. They are fronts for demonic activity.

The environment of Athens had an effect on Paul's spiritual emotions. His spirit sensed the presence of spiritual beings and was "provoked" by the demonic activity associated with all the idols worshiped in the city.

An Event of Massive Sin

One Sunday in April 2007, our morning worship was heavy and depressing. A reliable couple in our church interpreted our uncharacteristic emotions as something associated with the spirit of death. Another reliable person in the service confirmed that word. None of those three people had ever given a word like that before.

Corporately, we prayed for people who were traveling. We also prayed concerning specific strongholds and then proceeded with the service without experiencing any significant breakthrough. The next day was Monday, April 16, the day thirty-three people were killed on the Virginia Tech campus only a few miles away from our church. Thankfully, none of the students or staff of VA Tech who attend our church were hurt in the incident. There is no doubt in my mind that the spiritual emotion all of us sensed that Sunday morning correlated to the events of the following day.

An event of massive sin can cause a super-charged spiritual environment in a country, state, city, town, building, or area. This in turn causes spiritual emotions to rise up in people who are in or associated with that location geographically. Paul could sense the sin of the Athenians' idolatry; the sin was what provoked him.

The danger is becoming desensitized to the spiritual oppression in a country, state, city, or town, which can happen when the spiritual oppression is long term. Leaders and other people who live in the area begin not to notice that something is amiss. This is why it can be good to bring someone in from the outside to communicate what is happening in your spiritual environment. That "outside" person may be able to see more clearly into your environment simply because he or she doesn't live in that environment and, therefore, is sensitive to it.

The Environment of Another Person

We can also experience a spiritual emotion from an event in someone else's environment. We could be picking up on a problem or a success in another person's life, and the sorrow of that situation, for instance, causes pain within our spirits.

When Jesus was facing His impending death and Judas' betrayal, His spirit became troubled: *"When Jesus had said this, He became troubled in spirit, and testified and said, 'Truly, truly, I say to you, that one of you will betray Me'"* (John 13:21). The emotion of sorrow was strong enough on Jesus to create an environment in which His disciples later fell asleep *"from sorrow."*[3] The disciples' sorrow in that moment was not their own sorrow — they were sensing Jesus' emotional pain. They did not fully understand what was happening until after their Lord and Master had been raised from the dead.

Strong leaders create a spiritual environment that can be sensed. This type of phenomenon occurs when a person who is a gifted leader has an authority to influence others. That authority will create a spiritual environment that will either be used to serve others in godliness or to influence them toward deception and enslavement. When John says to test the spirit of a prophet, he is talking about sensing the environment created by that prophet or leader.

The Environment of a Group of People

One Sunday during our worship service, one of our intercessors started feeling hopeless. She ruled out that she was feeling a soulish emotion because she was not entertaining any thoughts or conclusions that would encourage her to feel that way. The Lord led her to walk out the front door of the church. The farther she walked from the sanctuary, the less hopelessness she felt, but when she walked back toward the sanctuary, the feeling increased. She shared what she was feeling with another leader and me, and we were able to address strongholds of hopelessness in the church.

A house or church can create a spiritual environment that can be emotionally sensed. We know that Jesus experienced the spiritual emotion of grief when He went to Mary and Martha's house after Lazarus' death. The sorrow of the people present created a spiritual environment of sorrow and grief that caused Jesus to become spiritually provoked.[4]

After the April 16 tragedy at Virginia Tech, a campus minister told me how the students were tired all the time. We talked about how Jesus' sorrow in the garden created a spiritual environment that caused the disciples to fall asleep.[5] I believe the campus minister was witnessing the same thing. The sorrow of the shooting created a spiritual environment of sorrow, which produced in the students an abnormal desire for sleep.

I use spiritual emotions to discern the spiritual atmosphere of meetings I attend as well as the meetings I am responsible for. When I sense confusion and disorder in a meeting, for example, it signals to me that we need to pray. We can confidently use spiritual emotions to discern the spiritual environments of our churches, homes, communities, and even countries.

Positive Spiritual Emotions

Up until this point, we have talked about how a spiritual environment can cause sorrowful or grievous spiritual emotions. An environment can also produce positive spiritual emotions like joy and love. Remember that spiritual emotions are the fruit of the Spirit. Psalm 21:6 tells us that the fruit of the Spirit is found in the spiritual environment of God's presence, manifested in the fullness of joy.

God gave us an awesome privilege when He created us in such a way that we can feel the reality of His presence. The spiritual environment of His presence not only generates love, joy, peace, patience, etc., but it can produce many other types of emotions as well, such as fear, reverence, and awe. I have heard testimonies of churches that were walking in such unity and vision that they changed their community's spiritual environment.

So in summary, we can experience emotions that are generated by the spiritual environment surrounding us. Some environments are created by God's presence. Some are caused by demonic activity, and some are the result of human activity. Either way, it is very important for us to be able to discern the origin of the event or environment our spirits are sensing.

Sensing Events in Other People

Finally, we can receive information with our spirits through our interactions with other people. We can spiritually discern what is happening in their lives.

In Mark 2:6–8, Jesus spiritually discerned the conclusions of the scribes' hearts (emphasis added):

> "But some of the scribes were sitting there and reasoning in their hearts, 'Why does this man speak that way? He is blaspheming; who can forgive sins but God alone?' Immediately Jesus, aware in His spirit that they were reasoning that way within themselves, said to them, 'Why are you reasoning about these things in your hearts?'"

We could say, "This is Jesus—of course His spirit could discern these things." But remember that He emptied Himself and lived and operated in the tools we can use today.[6] This passage in Mark shows us something we are able to do when our spiritual senses are developed and trained. Like Jesus, we can feel in our spirits what is going on in other people.

I was teaching a workshop on the Spirit-led life when the Lord instructed me to ask a woman in the session what she was feeling. She replied that she was feeling anxious, but when I asked her if there was anything she was anxious about, she said, "No."

I then asked who in the meeting was struggling with anxiety at that moment. A woman sitting beside the first woman confessed that she was. We started to minister to her, and by the end of our time that evening, four people were powerfully touched by God.

The first woman felt what was going on in the woman next to her. I have done that little exercise many times, and often, the person I single out will tell me the emotions of a person sitting nearby. This provides an opportunity to minister to everyone who is in need.

Discerning Spirits

One of the Holy Spirit's gifts is the discerning of spirits.[7] It is the ability to divide out the spirit of a situation, place, or person. We can use this gift to learn what is happening around us in the spiritual realm.

Whenever we use a gift of the Spirit, it is not the human spirit at work; it is the Holy Spirit working in us. There is a fine line between the two spirits,[8] but for our purposes in this book, it is important for us to know that our spirits alone can develop a spiritual sensitivity to discern, or receive, information. When we feel something in the spiritual realm, we are not necessarily using a gift of the Spirit; our spirits are simply doing what God created them to do.

When James and John wanted to call down fire on the people who did not receive Jesus, Jesus challenged the type of spirit they were operating in:

> *"But they did not receive Him, because He was traveling toward Jerusalem. When His disciples James and John saw this, they said, 'Lord, do You want us to command fire to come down from heaven and consume them?' But He turned and rebuked them, and said, **'You do not know what kind of spirit you are of**; for the Son of Man did*

*not come to destroy men's lives, but to save them.' And
they went on to another village."*

— Luke 9:53–56, (emphasis added)

Remember that we are to test spirits to see whether or not they are from God.[9] We can tell if people are attempting to deceive or manipulate us by their spirits and the fruit they bear. The emotional "signal" of wisdom from God is peace and gentleness, while the wisdom that is earthly, soulish, or demonic will emit the signals of disorder and evil. Remember Hebrews 5:14, which tells us that we have our senses trained to discern good from evil through practice. We need to pay attention and practice spiritual discernment in the small events of our lives so that when something major comes along, it is not too great a leap in our abilities.

Key Points of Chapter 10

I was in a counseling session some years ago, and I began to feel an overwhelming need to go to sleep. I had slept well the night before and knew I was not tired. I fought it for a few moments and then realized that what I was feeling was not me — it was the person I was counseling. The feeling showed me that she was dealing with a spirit of sorrow, which was making her tired. So I redirected our conversation and asked her if she was struggling with sorrow in any area of her life. As it turned out, she was. My spirit was picking up on what was occurring in her, and as a result, she was able to receive ministry in that specific area. The Lord set her free from that pain.

Just about everyone understands the five physical senses God has created us with, but it has been my experience that very few of us understand the different ways we can sense things in the spiritual realm through our spirits. When we understand the function and operation of our spirits, we can experience so much more in the spiritual realm, especially concerning the ways of God.

The human spirit is a communication link through which we can feel and receive information. In this chapter, we looked at four external sources our spirits can sense and feel:

1. We can feel and receive things from God.
2. We can feel the presence of spiritual beings.
3. We can feel spiritual environments.
4. We can discern what is going on in other people.

We can learn to use the senses the Lord has given us to discern good from evil. Up until now, we have looked at how our spirits can sense events outside of us in the spiritual realm. In the next chapter, we are going to examine the feeling of spiritual events occurring inside of us.

Notes / Reference Scriptures

1. Psalm 126
2. Romans 15:33
3. Luke 22:44-45
4. John 11:33
5. Luke 22:45
6. Philippians 2:5-8
7. 1 Corinthians 12:10
8. 1 Corinthians 6:17
9. 1 John 4:1-3

Coloring Inside the Lines: How Internal Events Can Cause Spiritual Emotions

One night many years ago, I was lying in bed quietly worshiping God with all of my heart. Paula was asleep next to me. As I poured out my adorations of love for Him and His goodness, all of a sudden, I felt His power come over me and fill me with unexplainable and overwhelming joy. Without meaning to, I began to pray in the spirit. I just lay there filled with power and joy. This was the first time God baptized me and filled me with the reality of His Holy Spirit.

Even though that experience with God was unique, I since have had many awesome and inspiring encounters with Him. Theologically, I call these experiences being *"filled with the Spirit"* (Ephesians 5:18–19). I cannot focus my heart on God and His nature and character without being filled with His Spirit. The measure of those fillings varies, but with every one, I can feel the fruit of His Spirit permeating my heart and soul.

Internal spiritual emotions are a little more complex than external spiritual emotions. The complexity begins with the reality that three different spiritual sources can signal events within us. These sources are the Person of the Holy Spirit, our own spirits, and demonic spirits. Each of these sources can signal a spiritual event that occurred in the past, is occurring now, or will occur. A source itself can signal something just by being there. We can feel these sources within us, and we need to understand how the subsequent emotions can affect our lives.

The Holy Spirit

The first source of an internal spiritual event is the Person of the Holy Spirit. For believers in Jesus Christ, the Holy Spirit lives and dwells within our bodies. He is not an unfeeling, deaf, mute, impersonal spiritual force but a living Being.

The Holy Spirit Feels

> "*The earth was formless and void, and darkness was over the surface of the deep, and the Spirit of God was moving [brooding like a mother hen] over the surface of the waters.*" — Genesis 1:2

> "*Do not **grieve the Holy Spirit of God**, by whom you were sealed for the day of redemption.*" — Ephesians 4:30, (emphasis added)

> "*But they rebelled, and **grieved** His Holy Spirit.*" — Isaiah 63:10, (emphasis added)

The Holy Spirit is a personal Being with emotions. His emotions are so important that there are scriptural warnings about violating them. The Holy Spirit is sensitive to what is going on in us and around us. When we align our lives with His sensitivity, we can walk in blessing and avoid needless pain and sorrow. The Holy Spirit is always willing to communicate with us what He is feeling.

The Holy Spirit Hears and Speaks

> *"But when He, the Spirit of truth, comes, He will guide you into all the truth; for He will not **speak** on His own initiative, but whatever **He hears, He will speak**; and He will disclose to you what is to come."*
> — John 16:13, (emphasis added)

> *"Then the Spirit said to Philip, 'Go up and join this chariot.'"* — Acts 8:29

> *"While they were ministering to the Lord and fasting, the Holy Spirit said, 'Set apart for Me Barnabas and Saul for the work to which I have called them.'"* — Acts 13:2

The Holy Spirit is a living, divine spiritual Being who hears, speaks, and feels. Because He has these abilities and characteristics, whatever and whenever He is speaking, hearing, and feeling, we will sense His actions and emotions within us. When we are born again, our spirits and the Holy Spirit become linked together, so what our spirits feel, the Holy Spirit feels. What the Holy Spirit feels, our spirits feel. Our connection to the Holy Spirit provides us with a phenomenal resource. Just think about it — we are connected to all of the very nature of God!

Because of the connection and close relationship between the Holy Spirit and our spirits, we can feel His guidance and prompting, which enables us to live in a way that is completely in line with His will.

The Human Spirit

When we are born again, our spirits take on the Holy Spirit's nature. Notice in the following passages how the characteristics of God become the characteristics of our spirits:

> *"For God has not given us a spirit of timidity, but of power and love and discipline."*   — 2 Timothy 1:7

> *"Put on the new self [the spirit], which in the likeness of God has been created in righteousness and holiness of the truth."*   — Ephesians 4:24

When we are "born from above," it is a spiritual rebirth.[1] Our spirits become holy and righteous, and they are conformed to the image of God. We are "renewed to a true knowledge according to the image of the One who created" us.[2] Whenever we talk about emotions occurring within our spirits, we are talking about the spiritual emotions of the Holy Spirit, because our spirits and the Holy Spirit have the same character. Paul's spirit was fully redeemed, which was why it felt provoked by the idolatry in Athens.[3] What the Holy Spirit was feeling in that instance, Paul's spirit was also feeling.

We can trust the emotions of our spirits because they are in the likeness of God. Both Romans 8:4–6 and Galatians 5:16–23 talk about walking in the Spirit, but neither of those passages specifies whose spirit. We cannot tell whether Paul meant walking in the Holy Spirit or walking in the resources and guidance of our own spirits. Romans 8 mentions both. My conviction is that Paul meant the Holy Spirit—but because our spirits and the Holy Spirit are one, it will feel like it is our spirits.

Our spirits and the Holy Spirit are one—they are "married."[4] Because of that holy union, when we, as spiritually born again children of God, are intimate with the world, we are committing spiritual adultery: *"You adulteresses, do you not know that friendship with the world is hostility toward God?*

Therefore whoever wishes to be a friend of the world makes himself an enemy of God" (James 4:4). We are to guard our relationship with the Holy Spirit, just as a husband and wife are to guard their relationship with one another.

The emotions of our spirits are holy and righteous. If the emotions we feel are not in line with the holy truth of God's Word, we can know they are not from our spirits or from the Holy Spirit of God.

Internal Spiritual Emotions

The Holy Spirit's internal emotions signal to us the condition of our walk of faith with Him. Specifically, the spiritual emotions of love, joy, peace, and the other fruit of the Spirit signal that we are walking in the Holy Spirit's resources and guidance. The fruit of the Spirit is the result of walking in the Spirit. It is not a list of qualities to attain; it is the result of walking with Him.[5]

Remember that there are not nine different fruits of the Spirit. There is one fruit with nine facets. The fruit of the Spirit is like a nine-sided box—all nine of these valuable facets, or signals, are connected to each other. If I have love of the Spirit, I will have joy and peace of the Spirit. If I have joy and peace of the Spirit, I will have patience. If I have patience of the Spirit, I will have self-control of the Spirit. The facets of the fruit of the Spirit are important signals to us that we are walking in the Spirit.

When I do not have patience, it indicates that I need to set my mind on the things of the Spirit, so I may walk in the Spirit.[6] I do not need to pray for patience; I simply need to walk in the Spirit's resources and guidance. Each facet of the fruit of the Spirit is an indicator of a heart relationship with God.

In the last chapter, I talked about love, joy, and peace being spiritual emotions of God's presence. We can externally feel God's love, joy and peace and yet not have His love, joy, and peace in our hearts. In this chapter, we will examine the spiritual emotions of love, joy, peace, and patience as emotions that occur in us. These emotions can be an empowering force in our lives.

With the external emotions of the Spirit, we are simply sensing what is happening around us, but the internal emotions of the Spirit actually empower us. When we become sensitive to the emotions of the Holy Spirit, we can experience a level of victorious living that is not possible by an adherence to religious rules. The emotions of the Holy Spirit empower us to receive the rivers of living water that Jesus promised to us.[7]

Love: The Internal Signal of Knowing God

Love is the signal of knowing God's heart. If I am in love with God and I love others, I am walking in the knowledge of Him. Knowing God, not simply knowing the details and "facts" of God, will always bear the fruit of love. We cannot know God and fail to love others:

> *"We know that we all have knowledge. Knowledge makes arrogant, but love edifies. If anyone supposes that he knows anything, he has not yet known as he ought to know; but **if anyone loves God, he is known by Him.**"*
> — 1 Corinthians 8:1–3, (emphasis added)

> *"Beloved, let us love one another, for love is from God; and everyone who loves is born of God and **knows God.** The one who does not love **does not know God**, for God is love."*   — 1 John 4:7–8, (emphasis added)

> *"But the goal of our instruction is love from a pure heart and a good conscience and a sincere faith."*
> — 1 Timothy 1:5

Again, truly knowing God does not mean embracing a set of details and facts about God. In fact, knowing Him does not even mean understanding and having perfect theology — knowing God means walking in love. The end result of the Word of God is love, as 1 Timothy 1:5 states. When I know God, I am loving God and loving others.

There have been times in my walk with the Lord when I equated knowing God with being able to quote large amounts of Scripture. But the reality is that to love the Lord and others is to know the Lord. As I really started to know His heart, His truth became like seeds of love within me that grew up and blossomed.

The revelation of God's love empowers our relationships, both with Him and with others. For example, His love enables our hearts to overcome the despair of disappointment, so we can live out a faith-filled relationship with Him: *"Hope does not disappoint, because the love of God has been poured out within our hearts through the Holy Spirit who was given to us"* (Romans 5:5).

It is God's love that flows through me to my wife, Paula. *"We love, because He first loved us"* (1 John 4:19). I do not have the capacity in and of myself to consistently love her as God created me to love her, but I love her with the love Jesus has for me.[8] My fleshly and soulish nature is very self-centered — but God's love flowing through my heart changes the intentions of my thoughts and actions. Every marriage has tough, dark times, and without the spiritual emotions of love, such a union would be virtually impossible. It is the love of God poured out in our hearts that keeps us from hopelessness when times are tough. His love in us emotionally picks up our souls and carries us through hardships.

Relationships with others can sometimes be a challenge, especially when those people are different than we are. His love enables us to have fellowship with people who do not look like, talk like, smell like, speak like, worship like, or even believe like we do. Paul tells us that when our spiritual feet are rooted (have a foundation) in love and we are anchored in love, we can reach out with our hearts to embrace the differences that are in the Body of Christ: *"That you, being rooted and grounded in love, may be able to comprehend with all the saints what is the breadth and length and height and depth"* (Ephesians 3:17–18). The spiritual emotion of agape love enables us to live with one another and not be disappointed in our relationships.

Walking in love enables us in such a way that fears are cast out of our relationships.[9] I can live in freedom from the fear of being abandoned when I know Paula loves me and I love Paula. God's love in us empowers us to live with one another in freedom from fear.

If I am walking in God's love, I have no fear of experiencing His judgment — I will have confidence on the Day of Judgment.[10] His love overcomes my fears. When I think about meeting with God, my heart leaps with joyful expectation, because I long to be with the One who has loved me — the One I love.

Without faith, it is impossible to walk with God.[11] Love is the force that allows our faith to work. If I am walking in love and I know God, the natural result is that I will have faith, because faith works through love.[12] We believe whom and what we love.[13] If we do not love a person, we will be suspicious and question that person. If I am suspicious of someone who has done nothing to warrant my suspicion — a person I am supposed to love — it is a signal to me that an area of my heart is not walking in love. Love is a spiritual emotion that empowers us to live life to its fullest.

I could go on and on about the connection between love and knowing God, but in summary, the one who is walking in love is the one who knows God. Love is a signal of knowing Him. I have known a number of mentally challenged adults who may not retain a lot of facts and details about the Word of God, but it is clear to me that they know God because they love Him and other people. The love of God flowing through us gives life to our relationships.

Joy: The Internal Signal of Faith

Joy is another crucial spiritual emotion that signals internal events. Whenever we are joyful, we can know that we are, in that moment, believing and trusting God from our hearts.

> *"For **our heart rejoices in Him**,*
> ***Because we trust** in His holy name."*
> — Psalm 33:21, (emphasis added)

> *"Now may the God of hope **fill you with all joy and peace in believing**, so that you will abound in hope by the power of the Holy Spirit."*
> — Romans 15:13, (emphasis added)

> *"Convinced of this, I know that I will remain and continue with you all for your progress and **joy in the faith**."*
> —Philippians 1:25, (emphasis added)

We can tell if we are living in a trust relationship with the Lord by the presence, or absence, of joy in our hearts. Trust in Him generates joy. Remember that joy is part of the fruit of the Spirit; it is the signal that tells us when our hearts are fixed on the nature and character of God. If I do not have joy, it is a signal to me that I am not walking in faith.

Joy gives us spiritual and soulish strength: *"Do not be grieved, for the joy of the Lord is your strength"* (Nehemiah 8:10). Because joy is a source of spiritual strength, when we feel weak spiritually, it is a signal that something is stealing our joy. And if something has stolen our joy, it has also stolen our faith, since joy is a signal of faith.

Peace: The Internal Signal of Right Relationships

The peace of God is the internal spiritual emotion that signals to us when we are in right relationship with Him and others:

"Glory to God in the highest, and on earth peace among men with whom He is pleased." — Luke 2:14

"If possible, so far as it depends on you, be at peace with all men." — Romans 12:18

The world seeks to distract us from our relationship with God. It tries to fill our lives with so many things to do and worry about, but if we are rightly focused on the Lord through the relationship-building tool of prayer, peace will fill our hearts:

"Be anxious for nothing, but in everything by prayer and supplication with thanksgiving let your requests be made known to God. And the peace of God, which surpasses all comprehension, will guard your hearts and your minds in Christ Jesus." — Philippians 4:6–7

"The steadfast of mind You will keep in perfect peace, Because he trusts in You." — Isaiah 26:3

"[Cast] all your anxiety on Him, because He cares for you." — 1 Peter 5:7

Similarly, the storms of this world are designed to cause anxiety, which can steal the focus of our hearts and minds. The Greek word for anxiety or worry (it is the same Greek word) gives us a word picture of "divided thoughts." The peace of God guards our hearts and minds from the onslaught of worry and anxiety generated by the world.

Peace is such a powerful emotion that it can be used to monitor and direct our lives.[14] As we briefly discussed in Chapter 1, the Lord teaches us to allow peace (another fruit of the Spirit) to be the "referee" of our decisions. In American football when a player carries the ball across the goal line, the score cannot be changed until the referee signals the touchdown with uplifted arms. The peace of God is our referee. If we do not sense His peace concerning our relationship with

Him or our relationship with a brother or sister, we do not have a "touchdown" as it relates to that relationship. The relationship is not right, or complete, until the referee of the spiritual emotion of peace signals, "Touchdown!" It is important for us to be sensitive to the peace of God so we can walk in healthy relationships.

Demonic Influence on Spiritual Emotions

"And this woman, a daughter of Abraham as she is, whom Satan has bound for eighteen long years, should she not have been released from this bond on the Sabbath day?"
— Luke 13:16

The third source of internal spiritual emotions is the presence of a demonic spirit. I have seen thousands of people set free from various forms of demonic enslavements, and I am continually amazed at the number of different emotions a demonic spirit can generate in a person. It seems limitless — different types of fears, different types of pain, different types of anxieties, different types of paralyses, different types of angers and confusions, etc.

But in the midst of all these things, I have also seen something amazing — the emotions the people experience after the spirits leave! Every time I observe this phenomenon of freedom, I find myself thinking something like, God sure is good!

I am aware that demonic torment, or what I often call enslavement, is a controversial subject. However, after thirty-five years of ministry, I strongly believe demonic spirits can torment, and even enslave, both non-believers and believers. Numerous Scriptures verify the possibility of demonic influence in the lives of Christians.[A] Paul talks about coming to your senses and escaping *"the snare of the devil, having been held captive by him to do his will"* (2 Timothy 2:26). Peter asked Ananias why Satan had filled his heart.[15] These passages and others establish that it is possible for a person to be impacted by the demonic realm.

Two periods of time are associated with the internal emotions generated by demonic spirits. When a demonic spirit has enslaved a person, that person feels an emotion that correlates to the particular type of enslavement. For example, with a spirit of anger, the person feels anger. With a spirit of lust, the person feels lust. With a spirit of hate, the person feels hate.

I have a precious sister in the Lord who used to be haunted by fear. As we were ministering to her, a spirit of fear manifested in her body, which, of course, heightened her fear even more. We lovingly and tenderly led her in ridding her heart of the roots of fear. When I commanded the spirit to leave, it did, and she began to walk in a new level of victory. A spirit was enhancing, or magnifying, the stronghold of fear in her heart. In fact, most of the fear she was feeling came from the presence of the demonic spirit inside her.

The second time a person will internally sense a demonic spirit is when that spirit is being sent out of the person. When a demonic spirit is cast out, that person will sense or feel something, typically in his or her body:

> *"But Jesus rebuked him, saying, 'Be quiet and come out of him!' And when the demon had thrown him down in the midst of the people, he came out of him without doing him any harm."* — Luke 4:35

> *"For in the case of many who had unclean spirits, they were coming out of them shouting with a loud voice; and many who had been paralyzed and lame were healed."* — Acts 8:7

The feeling or sensation will vary with the degree of the demonic enslavement and the type of spirit being sent out. With some types of spirits, the person feels only a release of pressure. However, with "extreme" types of spirits, there can be a significant physical manifestation.

In the reality of spiritual oppression, the spiritual, soulish, and physical realms are combined and become obvious.

When a demonic spirit is sent out from a person, the person will know it. It will be physically obvious to him or her that something has happened.

One time, I gave a prophetic word to a precious brother in Christ. Immediately, he keeled over as a demonic spirit started to choke him. I bound the spirit in Jesus' name and had my friend confess the sin that the spirit was using to harass him. When he had done so, I commanded the spirit to leave, and my friend straightened up, breathing freely.

"Man, this stuff is real!" he declared.

He was spiritually set free; he physically felt the spirit manifest and leave, and as a result, he intellectually came to a realization about demonic enslavement. This process affected all three parts of his being (spirit, body, and soul).

God's Moment-By-Moment Guidance

Internal spiritual emotions signal spiritual events occurring within us. Specifically, they are revelations of our spiritual condition. When I read a familiar passage of Scripture and it suddenly becomes real to me, I feel a sensation of joy. An event has happened within me; God gave me revelation, and my spirit rejoiced because of it. Anytime the Lord reveals a truth to us, we will experience spiritual emotions that need a response. Jesus speaks the words of God—so we can have joy.[16] If I stick my finger in an electrical outlet, I feel a jolt of electricity. If I stick my finger in the outlet and there is no jolt, the electricity is off, or there is something hindering its flow. In the same way, if there is revelation from God but no sensation of joy, something is blocking the flow of spiritual emotions.

Internal spiritual emotions can be used in our moment-by-moment relationship with the Lord. We can tell when we say something about another person that we shouldn't be saying—we can sense the grief the Holy Spirit is experiencing.[17] Similarly, when we see the effects of sin, death, and injustice, the spiritual emotions of sorrow and grief can easily begin to flow within us; we are feeling what God is feeling about that situation.

We can also use internal spiritual emotions to discern sinful events in our lives. Harboring sin cuts us off from the life flow of God. Isaiah 59:1–2 tells us that God is willing and wanting to act on our behalf, but our sins hinder Him from doing so, which causes us to be hit by spiritual heaviness. Conversely, when we confess our sins, our spirits are released into feelings of refreshment and freedom:

> *"Therefore repent and return, so that your sins may be wiped away, in order that times of re reshing may come from the presence of the Lord."* — Acts 3:19

The heaviness and weakness lift, and the life of God begins to flow into our spirits again. Processing personal sin is an internal spiritual event that will generate spiritual emotions.

In conclusion, it is important for us to use spiritual emotions to monitor our walk with God. Our God is a spiritual and emotional Being, so walking with Him in His fullness requires that we understand spiritual emotions. They are a legitimate part of the Christian life and signal events in the spiritual realm.

Most of the struggles we encounter are spiritually birthed. When we understand spiritual signals, we can live more enjoyable lives with God and others and avoid many of the pitfalls that the enemy puts before us.

Key Points of Chapter 11

Internal spiritual emotions are a little more complex than external spiritual emotions. The complexity begins with the reality that three different spiritual sources can signal events within us:

1. The Person of the Holy Spirit,
2. Our own spirits, and
3. Demonic spirits.

The Holy Spirit is a living, divine spiritual Being who hears, speaks, and feels. Because He has these abilities and characteristics, whatever and whenever He is speaking, hearing, and feeling, we will sense His actions and emotions within us. We can trust the emotions of our spirits because they are in the likeness of God. When we talk about emotions occurring within our spirits, we mean the spiritual emotions of the Holy Spirit, because our spirits and the Holy Spirit have the same character.

Notes / Reference Scriptures

[A] For more information about spiritual enslavement, visit dealingjesus.org.

1. John 3:3-9
2. Colossians 3:10
3. Acts 17:16
4. 1 Corinthians 6:16-17
5. Galatians 5:22-23
6. Romans 8:4-6
7. John 4:10-14; 7:37-39
8. Ephesians 5:25
9. 1 John 4:18
10. 1 John 4:17
11. Hebrews 11:6
12. Galatians 5:6
13. 1 Corinthians 13:7
14. Colossians 3:15
15. Acts 5:3
16. John 15:11; 17:13
17. Ephesians 4:29-30

12 Spiritual Emotions and Timing

On my first visit to Damascus, my good friend Emil Tarsha took me to the house of Ananias, the famous man of God whom the Lord sent to help Saul when he was blind. Saul, as you know, later became the apostle Paul. We could say Ananias set the spiritual direction of Paul's life and ministry.

I was looking forward to going to Ananias' house in hopes of sensing the residual effect of the spiritual blessings left behind by this man of God. But I was disappointed. The site had become a tourist attraction, and it felt spiritually empty.

As we left, Emil said he wanted to introduce me to a prophetess who was an inspiration to him and the members of the church in Damascus. She was blind, but she did not allow her physical handicap to hinder her. We rang her doorbell, and this precious woman opened the door and greeted us.

Immediately, I realized this was not just a precious woman. She was mighty in the spiritual realm. I became aware of the intensity of God's presence. She seated us in her living room and went to get us some tea. As she stepped out, the fear of the Lord began to fill my soul, and I repented of anything and everything I could think of. This was the presence of God I had looked for at Ananias' house. The Holy Spirit made Himself known to me as I sat there.

If a location has experienced a significant spiritual event in the past, we can sense the spiritual activity of that past event in the present. Remember that a spiritual emotion signals an event that has occurred, is occurring, or will occur in a person or in a physical or spiritual environment. One of the important factors in discerning spiritual emotions is the timing of the signal. In this chapter, we are going to take an in-depth look at the timing of spiritual emotions.

Spiritual Emotions and Past Events

On another occasion, I visited the ancient village of Gadara in Jordan. Gadara was the home village of the man whom Jesus set free from a legion of demonic spirits.[1] After Jesus ministered freedom to him, the man wanted to follow Him, but Jesus commissioned him and sent him back to his village to tell them what He had done for him.

There is profound archeological evidence of Christianity's influence in that city. One site I visited was that of an ancient church. It had a baptistery pool in the middle of the sanctuary. As I walked around this site, I could sense emotions of honor and reverence, and based on what I was feeling, I could tell that this was a holy site. I took the time to meditate on God's goodness in the past and His goodness in the present. Even though there was nothing going on at the site at the present time, the residual effects of the Spirit of God could be sensed. One of the most common spiritual emotions is the signaling of past events.

Unconfessed Sin

> "When I kept silent about my sin, my body wasted away
> Through my groaning all day long.
> For day and night Your hand was heavy upon me;
> My vitality was drained away as with the fever heat of
> summer. Selah."   — Psalm 32:3–4

232

In this passage, David was feeling "heavy," which signaled an unconfessed sin in his heart — the emotion emerged from a past event. He discerned the significance of the emotion and responded by confessing his sin to the Lord in the next verse: *"I acknowledged my sin to You, and my iniquity I did not hide"* (verse 5). It is important to discern and use feelings of spiritual heaviness to monitor any unconfessed sin in our lives.

Past Events Shared with Another Person

Spiritual emotions can also signal past events we shared with another person. For example, when David was fleeing from King Saul, he had the opportunity to kill him in a cave. Saul had been a thorn in David's side for a long time, but instead of killing him, David chose to cut off a piece of Saul's robe in secret.

A short time later, David began to feel that he had wronged the king. His conscience bothered him because he had cut off the edge of Saul's robe.[2] As a result of his emotions, David repented to Saul, and the king, overwhelmed that David had spared his life, called him his son and let him go. That is the reason Paul tells us in Romans 12:18 to be at peace with every person. The peace we feel signals that the events of the past are right.

Another Person's Past Event

We can also experience spiritual emotions from an event that occurred in another person's past. I am a father, and sometimes my spirit will receive signals of events that occurred with my children. I then can talk to them about what happened and use the event to help me minister to their needs.

One year, an intern at our church entered a relationship that was not very profitable for her. No one told me about the relationship, but as I prayed for her, I felt in my spirit that she had done things she had not wanted to do. So I lovingly and gently confronted her and ministered into her heart. One of my spiritual children was hurting, and my spirit received a signal of that event.

How Do We Respond?

With emotions that signal a past event, our response depends on whether the event was positive or negative. If the event was positive, we need to give some sort of expression to the event. Going back to the story I told you earlier, my visit to Gadara was an opportunity for me to give thanks and express my gratitude to the Lord for what He had done in the past. I didn't do this in order to live in the past, but I took the inspiration of the past and brought it into the present.

If the event being signaled is negative, most likely some type of ministry needs to occur. For example, the event being signaled could require confession and repentance of sin, either for something we have done or something done to us. It may require going to another person to make a relationship right. The signal could also be a warning of some type of curse that has been established against us, so we may need to engage in spiritual warfare. Whatever the event, the Lord is faithful to give us the wisdom we need to respond to it in an appropriate manner.

When we are focused on the Lord, our spirits can reveal to us things that need to be addressed or honored, therefore bringing vibrancy and godliness into our lives, families, churches, and even countries.

Spiritual Emotions and Current Events

Spiritual emotions can tell us what is going on within us as individuals, in the people around us, or even in our environments. Discerning the current events happening in other people is important for the Body of Christ. Jesus often used spiritual emotions to reveal what was occurring in the people around Him. When He knew what those people were reasoning or dealing with, He knew what to say to them:

> *"Immediately Jesus, **aware in His spirit** that they were reasoning that way within themselves, said to them, 'Why are you reasoning about these things in your hearts?'"*
> — Mark 2:8, (emphasis added)

Because He felt in His spirit what was occurring in the Pharisees, He was able to speak directly to the issues of their hearts.

When I am teaching or leading a worship service, I use spiritual emotions to discern what the Holy Spirit is doing in the service. Using spiritual emotions in this way is also important for ministering the Gospel on the streets — or even negotiating a real estate deal. Discerning current spiritual events is a part of living everyday life.

How Do We Respond?

We need to respond immediately to spiritual emotions that signal a current event because our response to the signal can change or enhance that event. Proverbs 15:1 tells us that a gentle answer turns away wrath. When we sense anger being expressed in a relationship, a gentle answer can defuse the situation. If we sense another person's sin and the Lord prompts us to speak to that person about it, we need to respond appropriately so the result produces blessing for all involved.[3]

When spiritual emotions signal a current event, it is very important for us to respond to the signal by asking the Lord for wisdom. That is always the first step. Once we understand the movements of the Spirit, we can respond in a correct manner. Remember that John 3:8 tells us that the spirit-led life is like following the wind. We cannot see the wind, but we can feel it, we can hear it, and we can see the effects of the Holy Spirit as He moves in us and in other people. When we are discerning the movements of the Holy Spirit, we are listening, feeling, and observing the effects of the Holy Spirit.

Second, as it is with spiritual emotions signaling past events, our response to spiritual emotions signaling current events depends on whether the event is positive or negative. If the event being signaled is positive, we need to express the emotion in some way. For example, if the Holy Spirit is signaling an outpouring of His power or a remembrance of our salvation, we need to respond in faith in order to participate with what He is doing.[4]

When the event being signaled is negative, we respond according to the Lord's wisdom and understanding. A few years ago, a young witch was covertly coming to services at the church I attended. One night my pastor sensed a spirit of witchcraft in the building, and he publically rebuked curses of witchcraft as the service began. He immediately responded to what he was sensing.

Later that night, the young woman called him and defiantly asked, "How did you know I was cursing the service?" His response cut off the effects of her curses and also led to the woman's eventual salvation.

A spiritual emotion signaling a current event requires an immediate response. If the event is related to a demonic spirit, we will need to engage in some level of spiritual warfare. If the spiritual emotion signals that something is out of order, we need to repent and put things in order. The Lord is revealing the event to us so we can either enhance the situation or change the situation. Whatever His reason, our response is critical.

Spiritual Emotions and Future Events

A difficult type of emotion to discern is a spiritual emotion that signals a future event. The difficulty revolves around trying to eliminate the past and present as options. When the church I attend was trying to discern the signals we felt before the Virginia Tech disaster, we thought the emotions corresponded to a current event. Our interns were traveling home in bad weather, so we thought the signal was about them but later discovered that wasn't the case.

In every city the apostle Paul visited, the Holy Spirit revealed to him that bonds and afflictions awaited him:

> *"And now, behold, bound by the Spirit, I am on my way to Jerusalem, not knowing what will happen to me there, except that the Holy Spirit solemnly testifies to me in every city, saying that bonds and afflictions await me. But I do not consider my life of any account as dear to myself, so that I may finish my course and the ministry which I received from the Lord Jesus, to testify solemnly of the gospel of the grace of God."* — Acts 20:22–24

In this passage, the spiritual emotions Paul sensed concerned a series of ongoing events. Because he knew what was ahead, he was able to prepare himself for the tribulations and not become disillusioned.

I have heard numerous stories and testimonies of people who felt an urge not to do something or not to travel to a particular place, and they found out later that if they had proceeded with their original plans, they would have run right into trouble. God used spiritual emotions to direct them toward or away from taking certain steps.

Some time ago, I had a strong urge to fast on a particular day. I did not know why. When that day came, I began the fast, and as I was going about my normal daily routine, a young lady approached me. She had a tormented past and had since given in to a spirit of homosexuality. She asked me to minister to her. After three or four hours of ministry, she was finally freed from the very strong demonic spirit that had been harassing her. The time of fasting sharpened and empowered my faith so I could hear the Lord and respond to her needs. Sensing His direction prepared me for an awesome ministry opportunity.

Another time, I was greeting people before our first service on Sunday morning, and I met someone new. He was nice and cordial, but as I shook his hand, the Holy Spirit impressed upon me that he was going to try to do something unusual during the service. As worship began, the spiritual emotions in me began to rise, and I warned two of our elders that something odd was about to happen. Sure enough, about half an hour into the service, this man made a major push to speak publicly to our body. We were able to minister into the situation with grace and mercy because it did not take us by surprise.

When we receive spiritual emotions concerning future events, it is often so we can be prepared to face trials victoriously. God also signals future events to us so we can take advantage of glorious opportunities.

Discerning Future Events

The first and best way to know if what we are feeling concerns a future event is to ask the Lord for wisdom and understanding.[5] Remember that wisdom is the ability to understand movements. According to Zodhiates, wise men used to observe the movements of stars, which is why the three magi who followed the star at Jesus' birth were called "wise men." In addition, Zodhiates states that the phrase "wise men" came to refer to people who climbed mountains and observed the movements of troops. When we ask God for spiritual wisdom, we are asking to know the movements of the spiritual realm.

As we ask the Lord for wisdom and supernatural understanding about what we are feeling, there are a few simple steps to keep in mind. Jesus told us that His sheep follow Him because they know His voice.[6] If, however, the Lord does not speak, my conclusion is that He wants me to be able to test and "prove" His will concerning the emotion.[7] When Paul says to test God's will or what we are feeling, he uses a Greek word that is also used for determining the value of gold or silver.

If I am going to test and prove God's will concerning a signal, the first thing I need to do is rule out that the emotion is physical or soulish. I do this by asking myself two questions:

1. Am I physically dealing with anything that would correspond to this emotion?
2. Are there any thoughts flowing through my mind and heart that would correspond to what I am feeling? (Are my thoughts producing this emotion?)

If my answer is "No" to both of these questions, I can move forward and begin ruling out the different types of spiritual emotions. Does the emotion signal an event that has already occurred? If there are no past events with which the emotions correspond, I can then start ruling out a current event. I do this by evaluating my current events and seeing if the Lord highlights one of them to me. If He doesn't, I can conclude that what I am feeling is a future event. Again, if the Lord has not directly spoken concerning the emotion and we have ruled out all other possibilities, we are likely dealing with a spiritual emotion concerning a future event.

This sounds like a long process, but it takes only a few seconds to go over these questions. All through the process, I am relying on the Lord for direction, discernment, and wisdom. When discerning a future event, the counsel of godly, discerning spiritual leaders is also a very important resource.

How Do We Respond?

When we have discerned that the emotion signals a future event, the next important step is to respond to the emotion. Obviously, the Lord is allowing us to sense the event for a reason. First, it could be that God is inviting us to participate with Him in what He is doing. Amos 3:7 declares, *"Surely the Lord God does nothing unless He reveals His secret counsel to His servants the prophets."* When God gives us the opportunity to participate in His work, we want to position ourselves in a manner to meet Him with that person, place, or event. I have experienced tremendous results after sensing a future event and taking steps to participate with God in what He was doing.

The second reason the Lord would signal a future event is that He is inviting us to intercede for a person, place, or event. In Ezekiel 22:30, God said He searched for a man who would *"build up the wall and stand in the gap before Me for the land, so that I would not destroy it."* We have the opportunity to respond to His invitation and "stand in the gap." When our church dealt with the spirit of death the day before the April 16 shooting at Virginia Tech, the Lord gave us the wisdom to pray for the people in our body who possibly were in danger. The frustrating thing was, we did not realize we needed to pray for the whole campus. To this day, I believe that if we could have discerned fully and prayed appropriately, the shooting could have been less tragic or even averted. The Lord reveals future events to us for a reason, and that reason involves life. He is giving us the opportunity to participate in the release of His salvation in our lives or in someone else's life.

The third reason God may signal a future event is to warn someone else of a coming danger. The Ephesian church sensed that trouble awaited Paul in Jerusalem.[8] The disciples spoke to him about what they sensed, but Paul didn't heed their warnings. Sure enough, when he went to Jerusalem, he was arrested and thrown in prison. Could Paul's imprisonment have been averted?

It is amazing to me that God would create us in such a way that we could discern events of the future. A loving Father, God continually wants us to be aware of the events that would affect our lives. As we discover how God created us to function, we can live in new heights of victory.

Key Points of Chapter 12

Spiritual emotions are not bound by time. They can signal events in the past, present, and even the future.

A Past Event

If the emotion is signaling a past event, our response depends on whether the event was positive or negative.

1. If the event is positive, we need to give some sort of expression to the event.
2. If the event is negative, most likely there needs to be confession and repentance of sin.

A Current Event

If the emotion is signaling a current event, we need to respond immediately because our response to the signal can change or enhance that event.

1. If the event being signaled is positive, we need to express the emotion in some way.
2. If the event being signaled is negative, our response will be based on the Lord's wisdom and understanding. If the event is related to a demonic spirit, we will need to engage in spiritual warfare. If the spiritual emotion signals that something is out of order, we need to repent and then put things in order.

The Lord reveals an event to us so we can either enhance the situation or change the situation.

A Future Event

As always, we first ask the Lord for wisdom and understanding, and then we answer the two following questions:

1. Are we physically dealing with anything that would correspond to this emotion?
2. Are there any thoughts flowing through our minds and hearts that would correspond to what we are feeling?

If the answer is "No" to both of these questions, we can begin ruling out the different types of spiritual emotions. The next question we need to ask ourselves is, Does the emotion signal a past event or a current event? When we are satisfied that it does not, we can conclude we are dealing with a future spiritual emotion.

Why would God give us an emotion that signals a future event?

1. It could be that God is inviting us to participate with Him in what He is doing.
2. He could be inviting us to intercede for a person or place.
3. He could be signaling a future event so we can warn someone of a coming danger.

Notes / Reference Scriptures

1. Luke 8:26-39
2. 1 Samuel 24:5
3. Ezekiel 3; Galatians 6:1
4. Matthew 11:16-17
5. James 1:5; Colossians 1:9-10
6. John 10:3-5
7. Romans 12:2
8. Acts 21:4

PART FIVE

The Complete Picture

*"A joyful heart is good medicine,
But a broken spirit dries up the bones."*

— Proverbs 17:22

We have looked at the emotions of all three parts of our being: body, soul, and spirit. In this last chapter, we will discuss how each of these types of emotions can affect the other types of emotions. Physical emotions can affect the soul but do not directly have any effect on the spirit, while spiritual and soulish emotions can affect both the flesh and the spirit.

13 How It All Works Together

One night, I was teaching a class on emotions, and a precious sister in the Lord came in a little late and sat down at one of the tables. She had just gotten off work, and she had brought her supper with her.

As she was eating, she asked a question, and she didn't realize until afterward that she had food on the corner of her mouth. When she did realize it, we could tell she was embarrassed, and I knew that the emotion was coming from a stronghold from a past event. An event in the past had formed a conclusion in her heart, and she was now experiencing a soulish emotion due to her current environment.

A few moments later, I asked her what she had felt when she had first arrived at the church that evening and what she was feeling now. She said that she had been physically tired and hungry, having just gotten off work. But she also said she had felt an emotional heaviness as she had come into the building.

Unbeknown to her, the church had experienced a tragic death only a handful of days before. The heaviness she felt was the spiritual emotions occurring in and around the building. She also communicated that she was embarrassed about talking with food on her mouth because of something that had happened in the past.

Next, I asked her to stand at a certain place in the room and then asked what she was feeling as she stood there.

"I feel anxiety," she said, "but there is no reason for me, personally, to feel anxiety."

Based on that, I knew the emotions she was feeling were not soulish or physical emotions—they were spiritual. They were not "hers," but she was picking up on them just as she had picked up on the emotion of heaviness in the church.

"Who in this room is struggling with anxiety?" I asked.

Two men sitting near her raised their hands.

The Lord allowed this woman's spirit to receive the spiritual signal of what was occurring in those two men. As a result, He used the following ministry time to intensely and significantly minister to both of them.

In only a few minutes' time, this sister had experienced physical, spiritual, and soulish emotions, all of which signaled different things. We were able to help her sort out her emotions, and at the same time, we showed the class how to utilize every type of emotion while ministering to others.

In this chapter, we will discuss how each type of emotion affects the others. Hopefully, this chapter will help you see the complete picture of how emotions work within us.

Soulish Emotions

A soulish emotion signals a conclusion or belief established in the heart. The emotion begins to generate when our conclusions or beliefs are exposed to a corresponding environment. Most of the time, our beliefs generate thoughts, which then generate feelings. When our environment uncovers a conclusion in our hearts that is a lie, it can generate emotions that are not based on truth. If the cause of these emotions continues, the environment will eventually push us into taking an action to cope with or eradicate that environment.

Our soul is like the fulcrum of a teeter-totter. The spirit is on one side and the flesh is on the other. The soul determines the operation of both — one side or the other will be empowered depending on the attention, or emphasis, the soul gives to it. Soulish emotions can affect both the body and spirit. Let's look at what those effects can be.

Soulish Emotions Can Hinder Our Spirits

"A joyful heart makes a cheerful face,
But when the heart is sad, the spirit is broken."
— Proverbs 15:13

As the above passage reveals, if the heart (soul) is bound up, the spirit will be hindered. If the heart bears emotions that weigh it down with lies, doubts, or worries, the person will not be able to operate as God intended. Faith is a spiritual principle — the focus of the soul releases the spirit into operation. That is why Jesus told His disciples not to allow their hearts to become burdened with heaviness.[1] God gave a similar exhortation to Joshua after Moses' death. Joshua was to lead the children of Israel into the Promised Land, and no doubt, he found it to be a daunting task:

"Only be strong and very courageous; be careful to do
according to all the law which Moses My servant com-
manded you; do not turn from it to the right or to the left,
so that you may have success wherever you go . . . Have I
not commanded you? Be strong and courageous! Do not
tremble or be dismayed, for the Lord your God is with you
wherever you go." — Joshua 1:7, 9

Whenever we face large obstacles in our lives, it is easy for us to allow our hearts to become weighed down with worries and fears. But God, knowing the effect the soul has on the spirit, encourages us to control our soulish emotions. In both John 14 and Joshua 1, He uses commands to express the importance of not allowing negative soulish emotions to hinder our walk with Him.

Positive soulish emotions, on the other hand, make it easier for the spirit to be released. A person who does his or her best to be thankful in all circumstances will walk according to the spirit:

> *"Rejoice always; pray without ceasing; in everything give thanks; for this is God's will for you in Christ Jesus. Do not quench the Spirit."* — 1 Thessalonians 5:16–19

When we pray without ceasing and walk with an "attitude of gratitude," we are not allowing soulish emotions to hinder us or weigh us down spiritually.

> *"Finally, brethren, whatever is true, whatever is honorable, whatever is right, whatever is pure, whatever is lovely, whatever is of good repute, if there is any excellence and if anything worthy of praise, dwell on these things. The things you have learned and received and heard and seen in me, practice these things, and the God of peace will be with you."* — Philippians 4:8–9

Peace is a fruit of the Spirit, and the fruit of the Spirit becomes a part of our lives as we walk in the Spirit.[2] We walk in the Spirit when we set, or focus, our minds (souls) on the things of the Spirit, like thanksgiving and prayer. When we operate in thanksgiving and prayer, we do not allow the anxieties and doubts of our minds to weigh our spirits down.

So in summary, soulish emotions can influence our spirits, but the Lord strongly exhorts us not to allow negative soulish emotions to hinder our walk with Him. Instead, He encourages us to be positive by exercising the spiritual emotion of thanksgiving, which will strengthen us spiritually.

The Physical Effects of Soulish Emotions

In both secular and Christian circles of learning, it is common knowledge that soulish emotions can impact our physical bodies. Even though there is a spiritual dynamic to the soul, the soul is a person's heart and mind, which tell the physical body what to experience. In other words, the soul has an effect in the physical realm through the thought life. Our bodies will start to experience the physical emotions our minds are telling them to experience. This phenomenon occurs through electrical stimuli in the nervous system and the release of various types of hormones and enzymes into the circulatory system.

In simple terms, soulish emotions come to life as our minds and hearts tell our physical bodies what to do in order to feel. Science describes the physical benefits of joy and laughter. The Book of Proverbs talks about how the joyful heart affects both the spirit and body:

"A joyful heart makes a cheerful face,
But when the heart is sad, the spirit is broken."
— Proverbs 15:13

When our souls are tormented with the emotions of grief, stress, bitterness, anger, hate, fear, or doubt, the effects on our bodies can be deadly. Millions of dollars are spent every year helping people "quiet" their souls so these soulish emotions do not destroy their bodies.

In summary, the emotions of the soul can influence and affect the physical body, whether the emotion is a positive emotion that produces health or a negative emotion that produces fear, stress, or grief. Negative emotions can cause sickness and painful conditions in the body. Soulish emotions influence the release of the spirit. If the soul's emotions are overwhelming, it can shut that person down spiritually. Soulish emotions are very powerful, affecting both the physical and spiritual parts of our being.

Spiritual Emotions

Spiritual emotions signal an event. We identified two types of events that could cause our spirits to experience emotions:

1. A condition (spiritual events happening within us)
2. An event in our environment (the spiritual realm around us) or in the environment of someone we have relationship with or authority over.

Important for the Soul

Spiritual emotions communicate to our souls through all three types of spiritual events. The effect of spiritual emotions on the soul is crucial for experiencing and knowing God's fullness. For instance, in Philippians 4:6–7 we read that the spiritual emotion of God's peace protects our hearts and souls in times of worry or anxiety (emphasis added):

> *"Be anxious for nothing, but in everything by prayer and supplication with thanksgiving let your requests be made known to God. And the **peace of God, which surpasses all comprehension, will guard your hearts and your minds** in Christ Jesus."*

That same spiritual emotion of peace can also be used to gauge whether something is from God or not:

> *"Let the **peace of Christ rule in your hearts**, to which indeed you were called in one body; and be thankful."*
> — Colossians 3:15, (emphasis added)

Both of these passages illustrate the link between the spiritual emotion of peace and the health of the soul. Conversely, when our souls lose their focus on God and His truth, we lose the peace that comes from Him:

"My soul has been rejected from peace;
I have forgotten happiness.
So I say, 'My strength has perished,
And so has my hope from the Lord.'

Remember my affliction and my wandering, the worm-
wood and bitterness.
Surely my soul remembers
And is bowed down within me."
— Lamentations 3:17–20

Joy, also a facet of the fruit of the Spirit, gives our souls strength.[3] Joy can be used as a barometer to let us know if we are allowing our hearts to trust in the Lord: *"For our heart rejoices in Him, because we trust in His holy name"* (Psalm 33:21). The presence of the spiritual emotion of joy in our souls is a good indicator of our spiritual health.

A negative spiritual emotion can also be an important indicator in a person's walk with God. On the extreme side of negative spiritual emotions, we find demonic enslavement, but any form of spiritual enslavement can be a major hindrance to our relationship with our heavenly Father. In most cases, it is a solid indicator that a person's walk with God is not in good condition.

Both positive and negative spiritual emotions have a significant impact on the soul and its emotions, as well as on a person's ability to grasp the revelation of God.

The Physical Effects of Spiritual Emotions

"A joyful heart is good medicine,
But a broken spirit dries up the bones."
— Proverbs 17:22

Spiritual emotions can affect our physical bodies in at least three ways. First, our spirits communicate with our souls, which releases programmed emotions that tell our bodies how they are to feel. So the spirit affects the soul; the soul commands the physical body to release hormones and enzymes into the person's physical system, and that person has a physical reaction to a spiritual emotion. As an example, when the spiritual emotion of peace is established in a person's soul, it can bring health to that person's body. When the spiritual emotion of love is released into a person's soul, the physical body can sense and feel the effects of that love.

Second, our spirits can affect our bodies without going through the soul. Spiritual emotions can become so strong that they bypass the heart and mind to influence the body directly. An example of a direct effect can be seen in Daniel 10:7, which we looked at in an earlier chapter:

> "Now I, Daniel, alone saw the vision, while the men who were with me did not see the vision; nevertheless, a great dread fell on them, and they ran away to hide themselves."

Notice that the men with Daniel did not see anything — the spirit bypassed the mind — nor did they experience any type of revelation in their hearts. They spiritually discerned a spiritual being, and that discernment came to them as a strong spiritual emotion of fear. As a minister, I see many people physically overcome with the joy of the Lord. They laugh, weep, shout, dance, or respond in some other way that bypasses the mind and heart.

The third way that spiritual emotions can affect the body is through demonic enslavement. Demonic enslavement can become so severe that a person's physical body is overcome and held captive. This type of physical reaction is especially common when a demonic spirit is being expelled from a person.

Spiritual emotions can have a major impact on our souls and physical bodies. Negative spiritual emotions, especially those from the demonic realm, can entangle and enslave us, while positive spiritual emotions can empower us and carry us forward in our relationship with the Lord.

Physical Emotions

I have a friend who is a Christian psychologist. A few years ago, he took his kids to an amusement park, and he sustained a serious brainstem injury when he jumped off a tram. It was live or die for a while. When he came out of the hospital, he was doing better physically, but all of a sudden, he started dealing with severe depression, which is a common but serious side effect as the brainstem starts to heal.

The physical effect of his brain healing drove his thinking. All these dark thoughts assailed his conscious mind. He is a Christian and a psychologist—so the enemy flipped it around on him and started telling him, "You're a psychologist! You should not be entertaining these thoughts." He started receiving the conclusion that he was a failure, and because of the conclusion, he strongly began to deal with suicide.

The malfunction was in the physical realm, so I told him, "Realize this. Physiologically, your body is going to be dealing with depression. Don't let that drive your thinking. Don't let it form conclusions."

As a result of the physical injury, his body was pushing him to think thoughts that were in line with depression. It was physiologically occurring. But he could keep himself from receiving the lie that he was a failure and allowing that conclusion into his heart. This helped him divide out his emotions and categorize them. I am feeling this, but it is not telling me the truth. So I am not going to allow it to cause me to conclude that I am a failure. He couldn't stop the thoughts, but he could keep the lie out of his heart. As his body healed, the suicidal thoughts waned.

Physical emotions can be healed, but the residual effect of believing the lies of failure can morph into soulish emotions. Soulish emotions of failure steal our confidence to draw near to the Throne of Grace, therefore keeping us from receiving the mercy, grace, love, and peace of God. The sense of failure can escalate to an extreme level and result in spiritual enslavement.

Fleshly emotions are a signal of an event in the physical body, and they are commonly generated by four sources:

1. A physical need, such as hunger or sleep;
2. A malfunction in our physical bodies, such as a sickness, injury, or chemical imbalance;
3. A physical process, such as a woman's monthly cycle or puberty in a teenager; and
4. Some type of stimulus, like physical touch or a drug.

Physical emotions are not bad or somehow "evil," but if misused or misunderstood, they can become dominating and addicting. Physical emotions can affect the soul, but they have no influence on the spirit.

Physical Emotions and the Human Spirit

> *"The spirit of a man can endure his sickness,*
> *But as for a broken spirit who can bear it?"*
> — Proverbs 18:14

In my understanding, the flesh cannot directly influence the spirit. Proverbs 18:14 implies that physical emotions—in this specific case, sickness—do not have much of an effect on a person's spirit. Galatians 5:17 actually tells us that the flesh and the spirit are in opposition to each other. They are forces that work against one another.

In Matthew 15:17–20, Jesus rebuked the Pharisees for believing that the cleanliness of the flesh determined a person's relationship with a spiritual God. Again, this seems to prove that the flesh cannot affect a person's spiritual being. Physical actions affect the soul, which, in turn, can have spiritual consequences (we will discuss this in a moment); however, my conclusion is that since the flesh does not have a direct influence on a person's spirit, physical emotions also do not have a direct influence on a person's spirit.

Physical Emotions and the Soul

Alzheimer's disease affects the physical mind but not the depths of a person's soul. This dreaded disease hinders a person's ability to communicate with the physical world, yet it cannot hinder that person's ability to focus the soul on the spirit instead of the flesh.

I watched as my brother, Bud, a strong man of God, died from Alzheimer's. His ability to function in the physical world became severely hindered, but when I looked deep in his eyes and talked with him, the same sweet man of God was present until the day he left this earth. The reality of who Bud was and is never changed. The "emotions" of his flesh had no effect on his spirit and the depths of who Bud was in his soul.

According to Romans 7:16–18, sin dwells in our flesh. Peter puts it like this: *"Beloved, I urge you as aliens and strangers to abstain from fleshly lusts which wage war against the soul"* (1 Peter 2:11). The appetites of our flesh "wage war" against our souls and seek to be god in our lives.[3] They try to dominate our focus, and the body can actually use physical emotions as a tool to direct our focus. We typically call these addictions. The flesh can dominate the soul through the physical emotion brought about by the stimulus of alcohol, drugs, etc. People who struggle with cutting themselves suffer under the painful control of the physical emotion brought by the action. These things are dominating influences that specifically target the soul.

If physical emotions are overlooked, ministering to the person's soul becomes much more difficult:

> *"If a brother or sister is without clothing and in need of daily food, and one of you says to them, 'Go in peace, be warmed and be filled,' and yet you do not give them what is necessary for their body, what use is that?"*
>
> — James 2:15–16

Even though James is not specifically referencing emotions, we can still extract from this passage that we need to be cognizant of the body's needs.

As You Move Forward

In many of the circles I minister in, there is a major effort to discredit and ignore the things we feel, but doing so is dangerous. Our emotions are so very important. What we are feeling is important. When we discredit what we feel, we end up walking in bondage.

My reasons for writing this book could be boiled down to two things: I want us to be able to understand what is being signaled in our lives—and then know how to respond to what we are feeling. Our heavenly Father's desire is that we would be healthy in all facets of our being. In 1 Thessalonians 5:23, Paul prays that *"the God of peace Himself sanctify entirely; and may our spirit and soul and body be preserved complete, without blame at the coming of our Lord Jesus Christ."* Understanding our emotions and how to respond to them enables us to lead healthy lives in every way.

I hope that after reading this book, you understand that there is no longer any reason for you to carry the weight of these questions and others like them:

If I were stronger in my faith, I wouldn't feel this way.

God is bigger than what I am feeling, so I just need to ignore this!

If I am not full of joy all the time, there must be something wrong with me.

I also hope this book has helped you realize that life with God is a whole lot more interesting than anything you supposed! Emotions are God-given gifts purposed to help us live life to its fullest.

"You will make known to me the path of life;
In Your presence is fullness of joy;
In Your right hand there are pleasures forever."
— Psalm 16:11

As you continue from here, remember that when you feel something, you always want to ask yourself, "What is being signaled and how do I respond?" You will be amazed at what God does in and through you.

Notes / Reference Scriptures

1. John 14:1
2. Galatians 5:16-22
3. Philippians 3:18-19

APPENDIX

Simple Explantions of the Common Emotions

Biblical Answers
to Common Emotions

This appendix gives only a simple explanation of the common emotions listed here.

Obviously, many of these emotions are complex and much could be said about each of them. It is important to remember that God created us to feel, and anytime we feel something, we need to determine what is being signaled and respond appropriately.

Hopelessness

> *"Hope does not disappoint, because the love of God has been poured out within our hearts through the Holy Spirit who was given to us."* — Romans 5:5

With the fullness found in Jesus and in the Holy Spirit's presence, we always have hope. One of the foundations for this hope is God's promise that He will cause all things to work out for good.[1] If we feel hopeless, it means there is an area in our hearts that is wounded, broken, unbelieving, or shut down to God's love and the truth that He will always work on our behalf.

Envy

Envy is called covetousness in the New Testament.[2] Covetousness means "to hold more" or "a longing to hold or have." It is the thought or feeling that tells us we have to possess something. The only person, place, or thing we were created to long for at an intense level is the Lord. Jesus is the only One we have to have in order to possess fullness.[3] When we long obsessively for something other than God, we have set up that person or thing as an idol in our lives.

When envy or covetousness enters our hearts, it is a signal that we are not content. As darkness is to light, envy or covetousness is to contentment. Contentment comes from experiencing the fullness found in Jesus and having an assurance that our God will never leave us or forsake us. He will fulfill our needs, and He desires to richly give us all things to enjoy.

> *"Make sure that your character is free from the love of money, being content with what you have; for He Himself has said, 'I will never desert you, nor will I ever forsake you,' so that we confidently say, 'The Lord is my helper, I will not be afraid. What will man do to me?'"*
> — Hebrews 13:5–6

> *"Instruct those who are rich in this present world not to be conceited or to fix their hope on the uncertainty of riches, but on God, who richly supplies us with all things to enjoy."*   — 1 Timothy 6:17

When we feel we have to have something or someone, it could be a signal that we have allowed envy to creep into our hearts.

Betrayal

The emotion that signals betrayal makes us feel like we constantly have to watch our backs. We feel like someone will unjustly hurt us if we aren't careful, so we have to make sure we know who is with us and who is against us.

These emotions are usually a signal of broken relationships. We probably were betrayed at some point in time, and in this case, the first step in dealing with feelings of betrayal is to forgive the person or people who betrayed us.

The next step is to realize that God will never betray us. He will always pursue us with lovingkindness. He will always respond to us with lovingkindness.[4]

> *"The Lord appeared to him from afar, saying,*
> *'I have loved you with an everlasting love;*
> *Therefore I have drawn you with lovingkindness.'"*
> — Jeremiah 31:3

We don't have to defend ourselves. Our heavenly Father is the righteous Judge, and therefore, He will judge righteously on our behalf.[5]

Also, feelings of betrayal can be a signal that we have betrayed someone in the past, and we are reaping what we have sown. In this case, we simply need to make right the relationship we have violated. Whether we've been betrayed or have betrayed others, Jesus can heal our hearts and enable us to live in peace with our brothers and sisters.

Guilt/Remorse

Feelings of guilt/remorse usually arise when we have thought, said, or done something for which we haven't fully accepted God's forgiveness. If we are experiencing guilt concerning our actions toward another person, we need to ask that person to forgive us.[6] However, if we have already asked the Lord to forgive us for a specific event, and we're still feeling guilt, then we need to rest in the fullness of God's mercy.

When I say we haven't "fully accepted" forgiveness, I am referring to the process of agreeing with God and forgiving ourselves. I often see people who have asked God to forgive them, but because they've concluded in their hearts that their actions deserve punishment, they hold the sin against themselves. Forgive means "to send out from the midst of." When we confess our sins to the Lord, He faithfully forgives our sins and cleanses us from unrighteousness. Our sins are sent out from our hearts, and we are cleansed from their effects.

> *"If we confess our sins, He is faithful and righteous to forgive us our sins and to cleanse us from all unrighteousness."* — 1 John 1:9

> *"And their sins and their lawless deeds I will remember no more."* — Hebrews 10:17

When we've asked God to forgive us, it is very important to agree with Him and forgive ourselves. As we do, we are purposefully aligning ourselves with the truth of Acts 10:15: *"What God has cleansed, no longer consider unholy."* The devil wants to con us into believing that we need to punish ourselves for the things we have done, but when Jesus died on the cross, He bore the punishment that was intended for us. The end.

After we confess our sins, God's heart is that we see ourselves as He sees us—forgiven, cleansed, and our past mistakes forgotten. When we receive the forgiveness of the Lord, we can go forward with confidence. The past is past.

Abandonment

Abandonment differs from betrayal in that betrayal is the act of a person turning his or her back on a friend or loved one, while abandonment is more about being left behind. As one example, a child who was given up for adoption can struggle with strongholds or feelings of abandonment.

When we are dealing with feelings of abandonment, we don't feel secure in our relationships. Abandonment causes us to be afraid that our friends or loved ones will eventually leave us. People with strongholds of abandonment often will be tempted to reject or abandon relationships before their loved ones have a chance to leave them.

Abandonment is like many other emotions in that it signals a past event. The root of feelings of abandonment usually grows out of situations in which we were abandoned or forsaken, so, in this case, the first step is to make sure we have forgiven the offenders.

We also want to repent for any negative responses to the abandonment, like anger, bitterness, complaining, hate, judgment, rebellion, etc. Any negative response to these events anchors the pain and lies of abandonment in our hearts. But when we rid ourselves of negative responses, we are freed from the pain and lies and receive the truth that He will never leave us or forsake us.

Finally, the devil will try to use traumatic events of abandonment to sow into our hearts the lie that God has abandoned us. It is impossible for God to lie;[7] therefore, when He promises that He will never leave us, we can take it to the bank.

God will never, never desert or forsake us! We can renounce any lies we have entertained that He would ever abandon us.

Loneliness

In most cases, the root of loneliness is a softened version of abandonment that signals points in time when we have been left alone. A common cause of loneliness is dwelling on thoughts of isolation and being alone. For instance, loneliness can hit a single person when he or she is entertaining thoughts of being single. It is important in moments of loneliness to hear the voice of our Father affirming His love and plans for our lives.

The reality is that the believer of Jesus Christ is never alone:

> *"Or do you not know that your body is a temple of the Holy Spirit who is in you?"* — 1 Corinthians 6:19

The Person of the Holy Spirit is in us, and He has promised that He will never leave us:

> *"He Himself has said, 'I will never desert you, nor will I ever forsake you,' so that we confidently say, 'The Lord is my helper, I will not be afraid. What will man do to me?'"*
> — Hebrews 13:5–6

Feelings of loneliness can also be rooted in times when we purposely alienated ourselves from others. In this case, we can ask God to forgive us and then receive the truth that our love for and relationships with others are important in His heart.[8]

Like other emotions, loneliness can be the result of sowing and reaping. We could be feeling lonely because we caused others to feel lonely in the past either by our words or actions. In this case, we can ask the Lord to forgive us, and He will begin to lift the painful emotion of loneliness from our hearts. Again, believers in Jesus Christ are never alone; we simply need to allow our hearts to receive the truth and feel the reality of God's presence.

Insecurity

> *"Therefore the chief priests and the Pharisees?convened acouncil, and were saying, 'What are we doing? For this man is many signs. If we let Him go on like this, all men will believe in Him, and the Romans will come and take away both our place and our nation.'"*
> — John 11:47–48

Insecurity filled the Pharisees' hearts because of a lack of identity. They didn't understand who they were in God's sight. When we feel the emotion of insecurity, it is a signal to us that an area of our hearts doesn't understand we are beloved children of the Most High God.

The truth of the matter is this: Jesus has given us the glory (the thoughts, opinions, recognition) God the Father gave to Him.[9] When we receive the truth of our identity in Christ Jesus, we will have the faith to speak and live with confidence around other people. If we don't know who we are as sons and daughters of God, we will sense emotions of insecurity when we are around others.

Sometimes the emotions of insecurity are a signal that, to one degree or another, we are living our lives based on the thoughts and opinions of other people. John 5:44 tells us that when we seek the glory or approval of men and women, it will cut off our faith. We were created to live according to the glory of God, not the glory of others.

Comparison, classifying, or measuring ourselves according to others will also generate signals of insecurity. Paul tells us that those who compare, classify, or measure themselves to others are without understanding.[10] In other words, if we compare ourselves to other people, we aren't operating in the glory of God for us. We weren't made to be like others — we were made to be who God made us to be.

In conclusion, when we sense feelings of insecurity, it is a signal that we are being attacked in our identity. We need to be aggressive as we seek out the reason our hearts are leaking the fullness of Jesus as it pertains to our soulish needs.

Grief

Many books have been written on the subject of grief. Grief is a normal emotion for us as we live in this world. It is a response to the pain and suffering of this age. Jesus Himself experienced grief many times during His stay on the earth.[11]

When we are grieving, one of the most important things we need to remember is that God cares about our emotions and the pain in our hearts:

> *"When Jesus therefore saw her weeping, and the Jews who came with her also weeping, He was deeply moved in spirit and was troubled, and said, 'Where have you laid him?' They said to Him, 'Lord, come and see.' Jesus wept."*   — John 11:33–35

When Jesus came to Mary and Martha, He already knew that He was going to raise Lazarus from the dead. Yet when He saw their sorrow, He wept along with them.

If we have experienced a loss, injustice, or extreme hopelessness that is causing us grief, it is important to seek help concerning the truth of the situation. In moments of grief, the devil will often try to distort and slander our understanding of God's character and heart. We need to know that God cares about our grief and that He weeps alongside us.

Anger

The emotion of anger can have many different sources, but it usually signals a real or perceived injustice.

> *"He said to the man with the withered hand, 'Get up and come forward!' And He said to them, 'Is it lawful to do good or to do harm on the Sabbath, to save a life or to kill?' But they kept silent. After looking around at them with anger, grieved at their hardness of heart, He said to the man, 'Stretch out your hand.' And he stretched it out, and his hand was restored."* — Mark 3:3–5

When Jesus saw the hard hearts of the Pharisees, His own heart was grieved, and out of that grief, He became angry. It is important to note that in His anger, He healed; He did not cause pain or destruction. When we sense anger within ourselves, we need to respond by appropriately processing it.[12] If we don't process the emotional signal of anger, it can lead us into serious bondage. Paul says in Ephesians 4 that it can give the devil a place to tempt and enslave us.

Anger can also be an emotion that signals a loss of control.[13] In this case, we want to surrender our wills and hearts to the protection and guidance of the Lord.

Worthlessness

> *"Are not two sparrows sold for a cent? And yet not one of them will fall to the ground apart from your Father. But the very hairs of your head are all numbered. So do not fear; **you are more valuable** [have greater worth] than many sparrows."* — Matthew 10:29–31, (emphasis added)

Worth is determined by what a person is willing to pay for something. In Matthew 10, two sparrows had the worth of one cent because that was what someone was willing to pay for them. But God tells us that He bought and paid for us with the precious blood of Jesus.[14] Our worth to God is the life of Jesus Christ, His only begotten Son. That was the price He was willing to pay. So God declares our worth in the sacrifice of His Son for us. He desires for us to receive His gift in faith, and as we accept His awesome declaration of our worth, our actions will come in line with our believing.

The world tells us that we need to perform at a certain level to have worth or value.

Feelings of worthlessness can signal a past or present inability to live up to the standards of the world, the standards of a certain religion, or our own standards. In this case, we need to forgive the person or people involved and rebuke the standards imposed in our hearts.

Feelings of worthlessness can also signal that we haven't received the fullness of God's mercy and grace concerning sins in the past. When we receive the fullness of God's mercy and grace, His view of our worth fills our souls.

Boredom

A number of possible causes exist for the emotion of boredom (an I-don't-care mentality). The number one cause of boredom is that we have lost vision in our lives:

> *"Where there is no vision, the people are unrestrained*
> *[bored]."* — Proverbs 29:18

God created us to walk in the radical world of loving others and loving Him. When we feel bored in life, it could be a signal that we aren't walking in the fullness of that purpose. A loss of vision could also be the result of fleshly passivity or immaturity, or it could arise out of a sinful, disappointing, or traumatic event. Numerous times in my ministry, I have experienced frustration and disappointments. If I allowed those events to sit in my heart, my vision would leak away.

First, we need to ask the Lord to show us what event (or events) caused us to lose vision. Then we need to process the lies generated by that event. Once vision is reestablished in our hearts, the boredom will melt away.

Another reason we can feel bored is that we don't have a clear revelation of God's nature and character:

> *"The people who know their God will display strength and take action."* — Daniel 11:32

When we know what God is doing, when we know the nature and character of this powerful, awesome God who loves us — the last thing we will feel is bored! David declared that God's lovingkindness is better than life.

Finally, boredom can also be a signal of an addiction to the world. The world is fast-paced and can feel frantic at times. We have hundreds of forms of entertainment constantly at our fingertips. People get bored very easily. I've found that God will sometimes just stop. He will be silent for a time, so He can help me allow my heart and mind to enter His rest.

> *"Cease striving [be still] and know that I am God;*
> *I will be exalted among the nations, I will be exalted in*
> *the earth."* — Psalm 46:10

When I sense boredom within me, it is often a sign that I need to wean myself from the flow of the world and allow the contentment and peace of God to fill my soul.

Depression

Depression is an emotional signal that can have many sources. Soulish depression is usually the result of lies that our souls have accepted concerning one of the following elements:

- A failure
- An external loss (the loss of a loved one, relationship, job, etc.)

- An internal loss of hope (the loss of something we have set our hearts on to fulfill a physical, soulish, or spiritual need)

It is very important to process the failure or loss in a correct and healthy way. We need to remember Romans 8:28:

> "And we know that God causes all things to work together for good to those who love God, to those who are called according to His purpose."

God does not cause all things, but He promises us that He will cause all things to work out for our good.

Depression can also be physiological. If we're struggling with depression even though we aren't dealing with thoughts of a failure or loss, it is likely physiological in nature, and we should consult a doctor.

Frustration

Frustration is the antithesis of the spiritual emotions of peace and patience. A common cause of frustration is walking according to the flesh.[15]

Personally, I use frustration as a signal to help me understand that I need to set my heart on the Lord. As I attempt to do this, the freshness of the Spirit of God starts to fill my soul, and the frustration usually vanishes.

At other times, the emotion of frustration is the result of our inability to do something that needs to be done. In this case, it is easy to begin to feel condemnation; instead, we need to receive the truth that we can do all things through Him who strengthens us.[16]

Notes / Reference Scriptures

1. Romans 8:28
2. Ephesians 5:5
3. Colossians 1:19
4. Lamentations 3:22-23
5. 1 Peter 2:21-24
6. Matthew 5:23-24
7. Hebrews 6:18
8. 1 John 4:7-8
9. John 17:22; Philemon 1:6
10. 2 Corinthians 10:12-18
11. Matthew 26:30; Mark 3:15
12. Ephesians 4:26-27
13. Numbers 14:1-9
14. 1 Peter 1:18-19
15. Romans ;5-6
16. Philippians 4:13

EMOTIONS CHART			
Emotions in the BODY	The physical body or surrounding environment	1. **Need** (Sleep, hunger, etc.) 2. **Malfunction** (Sickness, injury, etc.) 3. **Process** (Giving birth, etc.) 4. **Stimulus** (Touch, sound, etc.)	
Emotions in the SOUL	Beliefs and thoughts	An **environment** is exposing **beliefs**, which generate **thoughts**, which generate **feelings**, which cause **actions**.	
Emotions in the SPIRIT	An event that has occurred, is occurring, or will occur in a person or spiritual environment.	The emotion is signaling a spiritual environment or condition occurring within us.	

How Do I Respond?	Effect on the Flesh	Effect on the Soul	Effect on the Spirit
Pay attention to the emotion's origin and take appropriate action if necessary. Try not to allow the physical emotion to drive the direction of your conscious thoughts or push you into making conclusions based solely on the emotion.	—————	Physical emotions (such as lust) seek to dominate the soul's focus. If the soul focuses on the flesh and its needs, it can produce a level of death in a person's life.	Physical emotions cannot affect the spirit.
Is the belief being signaled true or a lie? If true, respond by expressing the truth. If it's a lie, deal with the roots of the belief.	Soulish emotions can affect the flesh positively (feeling peaceful produces health) or negatively (worry, anxiety, etc., can cause physical infirmities).	—————	Being controlled by soulish or fleshly emotions can hinder the release of the spirit.
Determine the emotion's origin and take action if necessary.	Spiritual emotions can influence and be expressed or released in our bodies.	Spiritual emotions and entities can be sensed, discerned, and expressed in the soul. Determine the emotion's origin and take action if necessary.	—————

For additional information on Emotions,
please visit our website:

www.dealingjesus.org

Made in the USA
Coppell, TX
10 March 2022

74788847R00155